AF556232

PROFESSIONAL STATUS OF PERSONNEL MANAGEMENT IN INDIA

PROFESSIONAL STATUS OF PERSONNEL MANAGEMENT IN INDIA

Dr. Subhas Chandra Parida
Senior Lecturer
Department of Industrial Relations
and
Personnel Management
Berhampur University
BERHAMPUR—Orissa

1997

DISCOVERY PUBLISHING HOUSE
NEW DELHI—110 002

First Published—1997

ISBN 81–7141–377–3

Published by :

Discovery Publishing House
4831/24, Ansari Road, Prahlad Street
Darya Ganj, New Delhi—110 002 (INDIA)
Phone : 327 92 45
Fax.: 91-11-3253475

Laser Typeset by :

Allied Computers,
Karnal (Haryana)

Printed at :

Efficient Offset Printers, Delhi--110 035

Contents

Preface

Personnel occupation in the industrial society has gained a distinct status of specialised management function. As a science and art of managing people at work, this occupation virtually effectuates all other managerial functions. Technology, market, structure and capital fail to realise their productivity without the human support. Hence, Personnel Management plays a pivotal role in modern organisational society.

That the personnel occupation has attempted to professionalize itself since its inception is evident from its history. The experience in U.K. and U.S.A. bear testimony to this. So, the study doesn't enter into the debate as to whether personnel is a profession or not. Rather, it evaluates the personnel "profession" as it traverses on the professionalization continuum. This starts with the would-be profession stage, moves to the semi-profession stage and then to new profession stages before being recognised as an established profession stage. Using an evolutionary approach, the study investigates the events prior to India's independence so as to denote the past personnel "profession". The industrialization process, growth in workforce, characteristics of the labour force, welfarism, trade unionism, legislative measures to protect labour standards etc. comprised the factors influencing the emergence of personnel functions and functionaries which are considered as small yet sure steps in professionalising the personnel occupation in pre-independent India. The further impetus these factors received after independence, along with improved discipline and training base, and the emergence of the professional body contributed to the consolidation of personnel profession in India.

In order to supplement the historical findings, opinions of the employing organisations, of the academic institutes devoted to the training of personnel professionals, of the trade unions who are dealt with by the personnel executives in course of their day-to-day activities and, above all, of the practising personnel professionals were collected through mailed questionnaire and analysed. In order to abridge the data gaps advertisements for personnel professionals were content analysed. The job title, job description and specification of the personnel job alongwith the actual functioning of the personnel executives indicated the inherent nature of personnel job. The extent to which training base is equipped cater for the demands of the personnel job is analysed by a cross validated data from different sources. The quality of the discipline base and role of the professional body in upholding the professional status of personnel has also been studied.

In evaluating the *locus standi* of the personnel profession on the professionalisation continuum, three parameters have been adopted namely; the degree of maturation in the features of personnel profession; the clientele served by the personnel profession; and the elitist status of personnel profession. After thorough analysis of the facts and opinions it has been found by the study that the personnel profession has not matured in its features to the degree demanded for qualifying as a full fledged profession. With an organisationally bound clientele, and virtually no degree of freedom in exercising the professionals' expertise role authority, the personnel profession is evaluated at as best a new profession. Similar findings have also been inferred with regard to elitist status. In arriving at these conclusions some comparisons of this profession with old and established professions like medicine and law are made.

However, the future of the personnel profession has been predicted as bright. It has scope for achieving the status of old and established professions specially in India. Such a prediction which is based on the recent awakening in India about the asset value of human resources, demands a few changes and improvements. The belief, as substantiated by the past and present status of the personnel profession, is that with its current position continuing the personnel profession may not find its place on par with old and established professions.

So a suggestive framework, in which the government, organisations, academic institutes and professional bodies are required to provide a thoroughly revised and improve support system to the personnel profession, has been advanced by the study. This contention stands contrary to the popular notion that, the personnel professionals singularly need to be held responsible for the current status and future prospects of the profession.

A legislative base to the profession has been sought on the lines of the medical and legal professions. Government has been called upon to take this desirable step and the professional body is urged to take initiative in this regard by acting as a pressure group. The logic for this suggestion, from which follows a series of possible outcomes influencing the discipline and training base and the inherent quality of the personnel job, has been traced to the Human Resources Development consciousness exhibited by the Government during the mid eighties. A country like India, which faces a short supply of capital, has to fall back upon its vast human resources. This is considered a strong ground for visualising a bright prospect for personnel profession.

While claiming no novelty, this study wishes to subject itself for further scrutiny as time passes. Because, it is the time continuum which has been the strength of the study that incorporates the past, present and future analysis of a promising profession.

Dr. Subhas Chandra Parida

Acknowledgements

I am grateful to Dr. Guru C. Patro, Professor, Department of Industrial Relations and Personnel Management, Berhampur University, my teacher, guide and philosopher, whose candid guidance enabled me to complete this work. I owe a lot to Dr. Bhabani P. Rath, reader of the same Department, whose scholarly and incessant guidance at every stage of writing the manuscript made the work possible.

I express a deep sense of gratitude to Prof. Gopal C. Rath, (Retd.), M.S. (Cornell), Department of Industrial Relations & Personnel Mangement, Berhampur University, who encouraged me throughout the research work. I am particularly thankful to the Personnel Executives who have responded to the questionnaire thereby enriching the data and making the study qualitative. The heads of academic institutions, the trade union leaders and above all the lone industrial unit i.e. Union Carbide India, deserve special thanks for their cooperation. I am thankful to the Director, National Institute of Personnel Management, who has helped me by providing the mailing list of NIPM members.

I gratefully acknowledge a sense of gratitude to Prof. B.S. Murthy, Department of HRM, Andhra University, Visakhapatnam, Prof. Anil K. Sengupta, IIM Calcutta, Prof. B.N. Shukla, Department of Laboru & Social Welfare, Patna University & Swarup K. Sahu, Department of MBA, Utkal University, Bhubaneswar.

My greatest indebtedness goes to Prof. D.H. Plowman, Director, Industrial Relations Research Centre, University of New South Wales, Australia & Prof. C.M. Muniramappa, Prof. Emireteus, University of Mysore who have recommended for publication in the book form.

It is a pleasure to acknowledge with thanks to Dr. D.V. Giri, Reader, Dr. R.K. Das, Senior Lecturer, Dr. S. Palo, Lecturer, Sri S.B. Patra, FWI of the department of IRPM, Berhampur University.

I am indebted to my family members specially to my wife Mrs. Sasmita Parida who are a constant source of inspiration and support in my academic pursuits.

I am also, thankful to Dr. P. Bisoyi, Lecturer in IRPM, Gopalpur College, Gopalpur on Sea.

Dr. Subhas Chandra Parida

1

The Study

Introduction

The Professional Status of Personnel Management is in debate in every country irrespective of the level of economic development and industrialization it has achieved. Some call it an emerging profession or quasi-profession, while others predict that it can never become a profession. Few see a bright prospect for the personnel profession. In the context of these varied notions, it becomes pertinent to probe into the 'Professional Status of Personnel Management in India'. So, this study, whose purpose and approach is clearly set out in its very title, attempts to analyse the history of personnel management in India so as to identify its current professional status and project the future prospects.

In this chapter, it is first attempted to outline the conceptual contours of the term 'profession' and the issues involved in evaluating any occupation as a profession. This provides a theoretical base for identifying the analytical framework of the study. It is followed by a short review of the Professional Status of Personnel Management in U. S. A and U. K. . This provides a frame of reference for India as it is greatly influenced by these two countries. Lastly, the rationale of the study in terms of the justification, scope, objectives and method is outlined.

Meaning of Profession

The qualifying characteristics of a profession have been identified at the earliest by Louis D. Brandies (1914)[1] as follows :

i) a profession is an occupation for which the necessary preliminary training is intellectual in character involving knowledge and to some extend learning, as distinguished from mere skill;

ii) it is an occupation which is perceived largely for others and not merely for oneself;

iii) it is an occupation in which the amount of financial returns is not the accepted measure of success.

In later years, more and more characteristics of a profession were added keeping the version of Brandies as the source. The list of characteristics as drawn from the various authors[2] is as follows:

1. Body of specialised knowledge with specific terminology and discourse of universe.
2. Skill for standardised practice obtained through training.
3. Entry to the profession regulated by pre-determined qualification, certification of proficiency and licensing of those committed to a life time career in the specialisation.
4. Service to the society as responsibility to be fulfilled in an orderly process and without solely indulging in self interest, thereby exhibiting exemplary self-control.
5. Community recognition of professional status and social sanction for exercise of professional authority.
6. An agreed clientele, as much as the clientele of the professional's own choice.
7. Organisation of the professional body with standards of ethics as the regulatory measure on the conduct and performance of the professionals.
8. Development of professional literature through research and study and sharing of such information among the members.

Currently there is a consensus of opinion as to the meaning of profession. This is evident from the semantic expression given to the term profession' by the Webster's Dictionary, as :

> *"a calling requiring specialised knowledge and often long and intensive preparation including instructions in skills and methods as well as in the scientific, historical, or scholarly principles underlying such skills and methods, maintaining by force of organisation or concerted opinion high standards of achievement and conduct, and committing its members to continued study and to a kind of work which has for its prime purpose the rendering of a public service."*

Issues in Evaluating an Occupation as Profession

Some typical issues emanate from the characteristics identified above which are relevant for evaluating an occupation as a profession. The first issue relates to the interpretation of features of a profession in reference to the aspects of professionalisation, professionalism and other related matters. The issues related to the degree of professionalisation determines the relative locus standi of occupations on a professionalisation continuum. Carr-Saunders and Wilson base their typology of professions on this issue. They categorise professions into the old, established professions; the new professions; the semi-professions and the would-be professions[3]. In the journey on the professionalisation continuum, every occupation traverses through all the four degrees of professionalisation and reaches the ultimate of being the old and established profession. Hence, it can be expected that an occupation striving to become a profession may face critics and barriers.

The growth of a profession is facilitated by its incumbents. It has been often observed that the professionals achieve greater degree of professionalism than the degree of professionalisation that the occupation acquires. This means that there can be a difference in the degree of professionalism that the members of a profession have achieved. A highly developed profession might have members who possess lesser degree of professionalism, as much as a poorly developed profession might have incumbents who have achieved greater heights of professionalism. Such paradoxical phenomena of either type is an issue which need to be concerned with while analysing an occupation as a profession. Taking into account the features of a profession, the issue that can be identified is that occupations may not incorporate all the characteristics in equal proportions. This indicates that an occupation might exhibit fully some of the characteristics, while being deficient in other characteristics. This condition is possible in case of all occupations striving for professional status and so, is very pertinent in evaluating a profession.

Further, it may be the fact that occupations in their anxiety to be recognised as professions may attempt to simulate many false postures of a profession. This is a condition which perhaps prompts critics to impose stringent qualifications whose compliance is strictly administered so as to restrain occupations from making false pretensions of a profession. As a result few occupations like medicine, law, engineering have been accepted as full-fledged professions. However, viewed in the light of technological advancements, concomitant skill developments and above all the increasing dignity attributed to any kind of work; the issue of thwarting the attempts of occupations to become professions need to be reconsidered.

The second issue relates to the question of clientele to which a profession serves. It has been seen in the characteristics of a profession that an agreed clientele as much as a clientele of the professional's choice is a basic requirement. Service to the larger society although is the primary purpose of a profession; yet, the target group of a profession's service is the clientele which is only a section of the society. Basing on the segment which is served, Gouldner proposes a dichotomy of professions into cosmopolitan and local. A professional primarily aiming at serving the cause of the profession is considered to be cosmopolitan and the one primarily serving the organizational interest is called local.[4] However, in either of the cases, the professionals serve in organisations. Yet, the cosmopolitan professionals with possibilities of greater mobility[5] and drive for high professional excellence, enjoy a better scope to have a larger clientele than the local professionals. Similarly, the scope for choosing one's own clientele is more for the cosmopolitan professionals than the locals, because the later category is bound by organisationally regulated clientele. This issue thereby reiterates the possibility of different degrees of professionalism that professionals may be achieving in the same profession.

The agreed clientele to a profession is conditioned by three factors, namely, (i) the approval of the professional role as crucial to the functioning of the society, (ii) the faith that the clientele as part of the society have towards the profession in general and (iii) the confidence the clientele reposes in the intentions and actions of the professionals in specific. All these above factors coverage upon defining the responsibilities of the professionals. *Premium Non-Nocere*, meaning "above all not knowingly to do harm" is the cardinal principle that elaborates the responsibilities of a profession.[6] The client agrees to subject himself to the professional's role authority because of the trust that the professionals will knowingly cause no harm. While the trust is important, the professional enjoys autonomy of judgement, decision and action, which cannot be controlled, supervised or directed by the client. The professional-client relationship is an ethical dictate ordained by the society, through which the professional while enriching the profession feels 'affected with the public interest'. Thus the profession's growth as well as the service to the clientele solely rests on the integrity and acumen of the professionals. Nevertheless, the role of the professional bodies as collective conscience keepers is important. These associations are culture sustained organisations based on colleague authority, setting norms and values to control the conduct of the members. The maturity of these bodies is an important parameter in evaluating an occupation as a profession.

The third issue relates to the evaluation of professionals as elites. Obtaining high status in society, profession groups tend to identify with that class structure of the society[7] which is deemed as the elite.[8] Taken in its broader sense, any socially visible category of individuals possessing some valued characteristics such as intellectual ability, high administrative position, moral authority (professionals coming in this category) consequently enjoy high prestige and widespread influence on others and are termed as elites. Bottomore's definition of elite, as 'functional, mainly occupational groups which have a high status in a society,[9] aptly encompasses professionals in this category. While professional excellence is as much important as the profession's service value to the clientele, the community recognition and social approval are nevertheless important in contributing to the elitist status of the professionals.

However, more than prerogatives attach to a profession; it gets bound by duties and responsibilities ordained by the society. Hence, the elitist status of a profession becomes contingent upon the social sanctions that elevates that esteem of the professionals to influence others in the society.

A negative corollary of the elitist position of the professionals is that it may create a neo-class structure which by virtue of its supremacy over others might get itself separated from other classes, thereby defeating the very purpose of a profession i.e. , public service. The role of the professional bodies becomes very important to keep the professional elites within the social bounds and ethical or moral responsibilities.

Thus, the issues in evaluating an occupation as a profession can be trifurcated into three broad dimensions namely, features, clientele and elitist dimensions. The study has reflected these three dimensions in its approach to evaluate the personnel occupation as a profession in India.

Personnel As A Profession : The Experiences and Observations in U.S. A. and U. K.

Personnel management as the function of managing people at work can be traced to the Arsenal of Venice during the medieval period of 16th and 17th Century.[10] With the advent of organised production systems like domestic production in 18th century and factory system[11] and resultant growth in industrialization by the beginning of the 19th century, practices in scientific management and employee well-being have been experienced in small companies of Great Britain as the Soho Foundry.[12] The New Lanark experiments of Robert Owen in England, the welfare efforts of Krupp family of Germany, the efforts of Leclaire in France, and those in the Textile mills of Lowell, Massachusetts and other New England towns of U. S.A.[13] were not only examples of paternalistic concern for people at work but also of the welfare movement (1800-1850) which is termed as the harbinger of the present personnel function.[14] The appointment of welfare secretaries around 1900, following the broadening of the range of benefits and programmes for workers[15] in both Europe and U. S. A., marked the beginning of the functionaries in personnel.[16] These secretaries were responsible for administering the welfare programmes. They were required to act as middlemen between employer-employee as the contact between these two lessened on account of the growing size of factories. However, there was no prescribed duty chart nor well-defined qualification existed for these secretaries.[17] Some personal qualities such as tact and common sense and knowledge of labour and industry[18] and flair for philanthropy and social work[19] were prescribed for the welfare secretaries. However, the institute of welfare secretaries was a short lived one. By 1912 the personnel department had started to emerge.[20] These early personnel functionaries were to look after the employment management. The functional enrichment of the employment managers was caused by the growth in unionism and labour legislation. Employment, education and training, health and safety, wages and salaries, employees services and employee relations came to be covered under operative personnel functions. Thus, the modern personnel function and the functionaries emerged in Europe and America during the 19th and early 20th centuries.

By the turn of the 20th Century the personnel function had emerged with a welfare orientation. It was the development of the modern management which contributed significantly to bringing maturation to personnel function. A pioneering contribution made in this maturation process was Taylor's Scientific Management Movement which highlighted three important personnel functions, namely, manpower planning, training and remuneration.[21] However, the early seeds of personnel thought as a part of management thought was shown during the 1830s, in the writing of Charles Babbage[21] and Andrew Ure[23].

Along the lines of development in the personnel functionaries and personnel thought, efforts to form professional bodies had started in U.S.A. and U. K. by 1912 and 1913 respectively. The Boston Employment Managers Association formed in 1912, and over the next five years expanded to other industrial centres. By 1918 the National Association of Employment Managers had been created. It was redesignated as Industrial Relations Association of America in 1920. Later it merged with National Association of Corporate Training (1920) and came to be known as the National Personnel Association in 1922.[24] Similarly, in U.K. the Welfare Workers Association founded in 1913 had changed its nomenclature over the years and by 1946 came to be known as the Institute of Personnel Management.[25] Thus, the first two decades witnessed the emergence and consolidation of professional associations in personnel in U.K. and U.S.A. However, it is pertinent to note that professional associations in personnel preceded professional bodies in general management in both the countries.[26]

The developments in industrial medicine created several new personnel activities like health care for workers, occupational disease control, workmen's compensation etc. Similarly, the impact of industrial psychology as an applied discipline on personnel function in the last decade of nineteenth century was of immense importance because it not only enriched such functions as job analysis, selection tests, rating scales etc. but also paved the path for study of opinion survey, morale, fatigue, accident proneness etc.. Further, the motivational psychologists with learning, reinforcement, gestalt and connectionist theories marked the beginning of behavioural theories in human resource management. The enrichment of the personnel function as well as the personnel discipline was furthered when the personnel experts borrowed general management tools and thought for application in personnel area. Thus, a body of knowledge under personnel emerged during the turn of the century which over the years became enriched by the influence of many disciplines and by wartime developments in personnel function.

As an expertise occupation demanding formal training, courses in personnel specialisation came to be offered at the collegiate level in the Oxford University, U. K. and in many Universities in U. S. A. by the second decade of the 20th Century.[27] Personnel literature in the form of text books and periodic journals also emerged at the same time.[28] All these developments in U. K. and U. S. A. by the turn of 20th Century cumulatively set the pace for personnel occupation to surge forward towards professionalisation.

During its formative stage, the personnel occupation was often called as a new profession.[29] Despite the enrichment in personnel functions during the First World War, the status of personnel as a new profession had not changed.[30] The emergence of professional associations and the outflow of professional literature between the two World Wars prompted Carr-Saunders and Wilson (1933) to place personnel under 'would-be' professions[31] thereby indicating that personnel was yet to gain the professional status, although it had a future. By 1943, Burk described it as an "emerging profession" and claimed that its dimensions were yet to be clear.[32] In 1950, Yoder discussed the trends in personnel towards professionalisation.[33] During the mid-fifties the personnel functions, the way they were operating, received as much stern criticisms in the writings of Drucker[34] as eulogies in the writings of Appley.[35] Both, however, highlighted futuristic improvements needed in personnel specialization to further its status in organisations as a managerial activity. Thereby, it was been established that the personnel function was yet to receive full professional status. By 1958, Yoder et al., contended that, "though the personnel executives are striving hard to achieve professional status; yet they are accepted specialists at the best". This is despite the efforts of the professional Associations and the outflow of rich professional literature emanating from research.[36] In 1959, Miller's when observed that, "the intrinsic nature of personnel management is such that should be a profession, whether its incumbents are now professionals or not",[37] gives expression to the debate as to the professional status of personnel function. Miller's contention was that though the professionalisation of the personnel function had taken place, the personnel functionaries were yet to gain professionalism.[38]

The early sixties also witnessed mixed opinion about the status of personnel function. While Reilley believed the personnel function was a "rapidly rising star " and was "one of the greatest untapped sources of opportunity presented by any function in management",[39] Wilking contended that "its standing in industry has often been uncertain and its course unclear . . . its status is dubious; its contribution, both potential and actual, has never been defined or evaluated".[40]

Ling (1965) on the basis of his historical analysis, predicted continued advancements on every professional front in personnel management, thereby resulting in general upgrading of the entire personnel relations function in the following two decades. But he noted a caution when he observed that, " The personnel executive will continue to grow in status and importance in the firm ' if ' he can anticipate rapid changes that will take place and meet them with imaginative programmes".[41] Similar view was given by Beach (1965). He argued that the personnel profession should continuously strive to train its members for higher standards of competence and to educate the top management about the values and contribution of personnel management.[42]

In 1968 McFarland observed that the personnel executive was striving hard to achieve professionalisation. But, when deprived of satisfaction over his work and failing to find increased status and influence within the company, he might turn to outside source for satisfaction. McFarland's view was that, the degree of professionalisation differed from executive to executive and the parameters to distinguish them were identified with the professional activities as opposed to fire-fighting role of the personnel executives.[43]

French in the late sixties observed that Professional Management and Personnel Department were in a state of transition. Despite the recognition and acceptance of the role of the Personnel functionaries by the top executives. French predicted new challenges and dilemma for the personnel executives in the 1970s. Behavioural sciences, organisational change, management, are some areas which pose the challenges and dilemmas.[44]

Rizer and Trice after an intensive nation-wide survey of members of the American Society for Personnel Administration, distinguished professionalisation and professionalism. Professionalisation has been linked at the occupational level and professionalism has been associated with individual incumbents in personnel. They concluded, that "at both the occupational and individual levels, personnel is lacking in a number of professional characteristics".[45] Ritzer, in 1971 revised this theory and believed that, personnel as an occupation would never become "profession, though individual personnel executives can become increasingly professional". He further suggested that the question of the professionalisation of the personnel as an occupation be dropped forever.[46]

The way individual personnel executives could go to the top echelons of organizations in U.S.A. was highlighted in the oft-quoted article of Meyer published in Fortune Magazine in February 1976 under the title "Personnel Directors are the New Corporate Heroes".[47] Meyer identified challenges that personnel executives face in organizations and argues that high level of competence worthy of a very senior rotative position in the corporate hierarchy is what is needed by a personnel executive to be effective. Thus, he argues in the American context that the industrial personnel executives can achieve high level of excellence thereby repudiating Ritzers contention.

The mid-seventies in U.S.A. witnessed similar feelings about the personnel occupation as expressed by Meyers. Miner, after conducting a study relating to motivation of personnel managers, concluded that "individuals with relatively high motivation to manage, who wish to achieve the rewards of promotion might find it advantageous to seek careers in the personnel and industrial relations field at the present time".[48]

Identifying the weaknesses of the role of personnel executives in organizations, Stanton suggests that by integrating personnel function with the total business, by enriching the specialist status of personnel, by promoting effective human resources utilisation, and by helping to solve organisational problems, the personnel can by virtue of his training experience and professional orientation be qualified to earn a better status.[49]

Despite a hopeful futuristic picture of the personnel profession, as depicted above during the decade of 1970, the common sentiment has been that the personnel professionals can rice in the esteem of others by their individual excellence rather than by their endeavours to professionalise the occupation. And Miner's contention aptly summarises the development of the professional status which reads that "some approximation to a profession are in evidence... A college education is typical . . . there is some sense of career permanency . . . Overall, the trend appears to be toward increased, but not full professionalisation . . . There is an emphasis on a common body of knowledge which is reflected in the accreditation programme recently introduced by the American Society for Personnel Administration.[50]

In the British context critical observations about the status of personnel profession have been made by Hunter (1957),[51] Watson (1977),[52] Legge (1978)[53] and Tyson (1979).[54] They have questioned the value of personnel management as a specialisation because the personnel specialists have failed to live up to their own claims as professionals. Such sentiments have also have been expressed in tho Donovan report (1968). The not very encouraging profile of personnel profession in U.K. has been attributed to:

i) lack of appreciation of personnel function as requiring analytical and personnel skills, as a result of which employment of amateurs is increasing;[55]

ii) disillusionment with the functioning of personnel departments in organisation thereby declining their influence[56] and credibility;[57]

iii) prevalence of inferiority complex in the personnel field[58] and as a strategic response to the felt lack of authority adopting a professional image:[59]

iv) failure of personnel management in U. K. to be relevant to the overall set of social, political and economic objectives.[60]

Tyson and Fell (1986) strongly contended that, more than the professional image, "the organisational context of personnel management is a crucial determinant of the occupational ideology, because the organization is the only real source of status and rewards. While commending the role of IPM in its attempt to professionalise the personnel function, they indicated that the IPM has not over-achieved as a qualifying association. Personnel specialists who claim a professional status alongside medical practitioners or lawyers do not find an agreed client. They firmly believed that the personnel specialists need not claim a societal status separate from their manager colleagues.

To conclude, the personnel function as an occupation emerged after industrialization. The most striking feature of this function is that, since its inception attempts have been made to enhance the occupation to the level of a profession. Yet full professional status is still eluding the personnel occupation. This can be gauged from the experiences of U.S.A. and U.K.

Rationale of The Study

Derek Torrington in his classical remark " the personnel management specialisation seems in a restless search of an identity, and there is not consensus on what that identify is" aptly expresses the nebulous stature of personnel profession. The experience of the two developed countries U.S.A. and U. K. aptly reiterates this contention. From a 'new' profession, before the First World War, the personnel occupation traversed through the stages of 'would-be' profession. 'emerging profession', and even faced the contention that the claims for its professionalisation be dropped for ever. Full professional status eluded the personnel occupation both in U.S.A. and U. K. where its growth actually started at the turn of the 20th Century. In this context, a study on the professional status of personnel occupation in India becomes topical. India as a pioneer among the developing countries has not only embarked upon large-scale industrialization, but also has taken strides towards professionalising the personnel function on the lines of U. S. A. and U. K. By attempting to investigate the historical origins, growth patterns and current status of the personnel profession in India, this study tries to evaluate its future prospectus. This attempt justifies the thesis title. The next section outlines the scope and objectives of the study.

Scope and Objectives

This study attempts to cover the whole of India. At the first instance, would appear quite ambitious, but when viewed in the narrow perspective of evaluating personnel as a profession, the coverage of the whole country appears quite logical. For example the studies made by Rizer and Trice in U. S. A. and by Tyson and Fell in U. K. cover a sample drawn from the whole of the respective nations. In India, studies made by Jacob and NIPM also resort to an all India level coverage. Besides such emulation appearing reasonable, there are some concrete reasons for covering a whole country to evaluate the profession status of an occupation.

The existence of a profession is a 'holistic' phenomena. In its features, as well as in its growth related environmental conditions, a profession presents the profile of a system which as a whole is made up of interrelated elements. Starting with the discipline base and ending with the ethical standards, the feature of a profession as discussed earlier are composite parts of a whole. Absence or lack of any one feature will not qualify an occupation to be a profession. Similarly in its formation, growth and consolidation, a profession gets influenced by the totality of social, political and economic norms, values and objectives. In this context, to limit the field to a region will be quite erroneous. Thus, the choice of the whole country for the evaluation of personnel profession in India is quite logical.

However, the personnel occupation as a post-industrialization development has grown only in the organized sector. Thus, it is in the manufacturing and service industries, mines, plantations, transport and commercial industries and such other organised sectors of the economy that the personnel occupation has taken shape. Hence the scope of the study is limited to the organised sectors of India irrespective of regional and other differences.

The title of the study is explicitly clear about its temporal nature. The history of the personnel profession in India is traced from the developments between the middle of 19th Century (i.e. the emergence of industrialization process till the independence of India in 1947). The present status of the profession is evaluated by examining developments from 1947-1990. This stage in personnel profession is evaluated by objective facts and subjective opinions. From the historical evidence of the past and current situation, the future prospects of the profession are logically predicted.

In the conceptual framework discussed earlier, three dimensions in evaluating an occupation as a profession have been identified. These are feature dimensions, clientele dimensions and elitist dimensions. The evaluation of personnel profession in this study also adopts the framework of these three dimensions, the justification for which has been given earlier.

As is evident from the discussions above, the scope of the study is clearly delineated. Yet, drawing hypotheses incorporating simple cause-effect relationship is not feasible in this study because of its wide coverage and exploratory nature. So, it is safer to set some objectives as guidelines of analysis. But in setting the objectives the task is not as simple as it appears from the title or from the scope. This is due to the complexity involved in evaluating any occupation as a profession. In order to simplify the approach one basic assumption is set out without attaching any debatable tag to it namely—

The personnel occupation by its very history has proved that it has attempted to professionalise itself since its very inception. Thus, the occupation has already moved on the professionalisation continuum.

How did the move start ? In what direction it is moving ? What is the degree of professionalisation achieved ? What would be its future ? These are all debatable questions which emerge only out of an acceptance of this assumption. The setting, of the specific objectives of the study becomes rather easy after this. The objectives are:

1. to trace the genesis of personnel profession in India covering the period up to the country's independence in the light of development such as industrialization process, the emergence of industrial work force, trade unionism, welfare movement, labour legislations, etc., having an impact on the origin of personnel functionaries and personnel discipline and to relate this genesis with the management profession in general ;
2. to observe the post-independence developments in the above mentioned areas as well as to highlight the discipline and training base developed for professionalising the personnel occupation during this period;
3. to analyse the role and status of the Personnel Officer inside and outside the organisation with the help of objective observations and subjèctive opinion;
4. to evaluate the role of National Institute of Personnel Management (NIPM) in professionalising the personnel occupation, and lastly;
5. to predict the future of personnel profession in India in the light of its past and present.

Review of Literature and Significance of the Study

Personnel management and its related areas have been studied in India both by the practitioners as well as academicians. Some of these studies are conjectural in nature while the others are based on field studies and empirical in nature. The conjectural studies broadly have provided a theoretical discussion on the personnel management functions and the role of the personnel functionaries in the organisations. The Indian Institute of personnel Management has also made attempts to study the personnel management function in the Indian context and to develop professional literature on personnel management in India.[61]

In the various field studies that are available in the published form, the scholars have attempted to probe and analyse the working of the personnel department taking the personnel practices as indicators. These studies[62] have been confined either to an industry, or a sector or a State. The development and application of the behavioural models in the arena of human resources management in the West have also prompted scholars in India to study the applicability and working of the behavioural models in Indian industries.[63]

However, studies in general on the working of personnel/welfare officer and in specific on the personnel profession in India are significantly scanty. The studies that are available in these areas are, a study made by Vaid[64] on the role and functioning of the labour welfare officers and another by National Institute of Labour Management[65] on the personnel officers. Besides, studies done by Alexander,[66] Kamat,[67] Myers and Kanappan,[68] though impressionistic can be added to the above studies, as these have analysed the role of personnel departments and personnel officers in Indian industries. The role of the personnel officers has also been highlighted in some of the studies done by practitioners.[69]

The first study, on the role and functioning of the personnel officers vis-a-vis the personnel profession at the all India level was conducted by Jacob.[70] The study has made a historical analysis of the different stages and land marks in the development of personnel management as a profession in India. The study has analysed the training, functioning and job satisfaction of personnel officers, based upon data collected from a sample of personnel officers chosen on an all-India basis. The study has highlighted the problems and the steps to be taken to make the profession progressive.

One of the recent studies on personnel profession in India was done by Akhilesh and Sekar under the auspices of the NIPM and India Institute of Science.[71] The study is based upon the data collected through a national survey undertaken amongst the corporate members of NIPM. The study has analysed the current trends and changes influencing the personnel function based upon four major areas namely, perspective and challenges; education and training; structure, contents and process of personnel function; and the role of NIPM.

The various studies mentioned above indicate that the present study has some resemblance to the study done by Jacob and the one done by Akhilesh and Sekar. But both these studies suffer from some limitations. Firstly, they are based solely on the data collected from the personnel executives. The role of the educational institutions in imparting training to the future personnel functionaries, the employing organizations who provide employment to the personnel executives and prescribe their functions, and the trade unions which interact with the personnel executives, have been ignored by these studies. Secondly, both these studies have analysed the role and functions of the personnel executives, the hurdles faced, the type of training imparted, the role of the professional bodies and the future prospects of the personnel occupation as a profession or the stage to which the personnel occupation has reached in the professionalisation continuum have not been analysed by these studies.

The present study, while takin cue from these studies aims to broaden its coverage. As an improvement over the other studies, the present study proposes to give importance to the professional dynamics of personnel occupation. Thus the study takes an integrative approach in evaluating the professional status of personnel in India.

Method of Study

Any research investigation makes it essential to select appropriate methods and tools of data collection. These not only facilitate collection of reliable and accurate information but also shape the analysis and final outcome of thé study. Presently a brief discussion is made with regard to the methods adopted for conducting the study, namely data collection, data processing, data analysis and presentation.

As has been mentioned earlier the present study is exploratory in nature. Resorting to an eclectic approach the study combines historical and survey methods. The historical method helps in probing into the past and in tracing the genesis of the personnel profession in India. The survey method was adopted to collect subjective data from a sample of personnel executives through mailed questionnaires.[72] By the same method both factual and opinionated data were collected from academic institutions, employment organisations, trade unions and the National Institute of Personnel Management (NIPM), the professional body of the personnel executives.

While the above respondents served as the primary source of information, the study also tapped various secondary sources of information. As part of the secondary sources, the research articles, reports and books available on the personnel profession helped the researcher to provide more insight Newspapers and Employment News for different years starting from the Year 1977 were scanned to collect advertisements seeking personnel professionals.

Data collection from the above sources were organised for the purpose of analysis and interpretation. Data so organised was subjected to both qualitative and quantitative analysis. The information collected from the advertisements in terms of qualifications, duties, functions etc. were subjected to content analysis in order to find out the expectations/ requirements of the employing organisations. Similarly the syllabi of different university departments, management institutes etc. offering training in the personnel field were analysed to find out the discipline base of the personnel profession. The opinionated data given by the executives was helpful in discussing the status of the Personnel executives and the functions performed by them. The quantitative data were classified and presented in tabular form. These data were also subjected to various statistical interpretations like averages, co-efficient of variations etc.

The data thus analysed has been presented in five chapters. The first chapter in its endeavour to introduce the study highlights the meaning of the profession and issues involved in evaluating an occupation as a profession. To get a comparative profile, the status of personnel profession in the U. S. A. and U. K. has been discussed. After outlining the scope and objectives of the study, the rationale, methodology, and limitations of the study have also found place in the first chapter. The second chapter, devoted to tracing the genesis of personnel profession in India covering the period from 1850 up to 1947, incorporates the factors like emergence of industrialisation, personnel functionaries and personnel discipline. The third chapter presents the current status of the personnel profession in India. The time period covered in this chapter is from the year of independence to the present (1990). The fourth chapter also discusses the current status of personnel profession on the basis of the findings of the opinion survey. The last chapter has summarised the discussions made in the previous chapters which lead to the predictions made about the future of the personnel profession.

Limitations of the study

Awareness of the limitations of the study is beneficial not only to shape the contents by bridging the gaps but also to appreciate the unavoidable lacunae in the study. Despite deliberate and diligent efforts to make good of the limitations, some data gaps, theoretical debates, analytical flaws do exist which need to be identified and justified.

In this study the main thrust is on the professional status of personnel occupation. The very purpose of the study will be defeated if a question, namely "can't the personnel occupation work like any other occupation in organisations without bothering to gain the status of a profession?" is raised. The question, however, becomes obsolete in view of the fact that the personnel occupation has tried to adorn the professional attire since early inception and in this regard it has preceded management profession as such. Since, the professionalisation efforts have been continuous since the turn of the 20th century, it is not relevant to raise doubts about its attempted professionalisation. So, this study addresses itself to the evaluation of the personnel function as it traverses on the professional continuum as an evolutionary process. Such a theoretical logic also justifies the temporal nature of the study, which is reflected in its very title.

For its coverage, the study appears quite ambitious because the personnel profession in India is under evaluation. But, in view of similar studies resorting to macro level coverage in U.S.A. , U. K and also in India, the study justifiable emulates them. The emulation is only to the extent of resorting to macro level approach. In terms of its information sources, this study has explored many sources namely the personnel executives drawn from the NIPM list, the employing organisations, the educational institutes devoted to the training of personnel executives, and the trade unions. In this respect this study distinguishes itself from other studies.

The greatest limitation was caused by the poor responses received from the employing organisations. Despite repeated reminders only one organisation i.e. Union Carbide responded. The implication of such poor response has been analysed in the study; yes, more responses from the employing organisations would have been better for the study. In order to minimise the data gaps caused by this, the contents of the advertisements made by different organisations seeking personnel executives were analysed.

The responses from trade unions and educational institutions, although relatively better than those from employing organisations; would have been enriched by a better response rate from some very important unions and institutions contacted. In order to minimise the data gaps caused by the inadequate responses from the educational institutions, the course structures of different institutions were collected officially on behalf of the Industrial Relations and Personnel Management Department of Berhampur University and their contents were analysed.

In tracing the genesis and present status of the Personnel Profession the author found gaps in the recorded evidences of events. Without claiming any novelty in this regard, the study tried to integrate the loose ends of the events into a meaningful display of the historical genesis and current status.

Resorting largely to descriptive analysis, supported by simple quantitative techniques, the study sought to be more intelligible rather than sophisticated in terms of quantitative analysis. This need not be construed as a limitation, because the study is largely historical, partly predictive and least of all is amenable to cause effect correlative analysis.

REFERENCES

1. Louis D. Brandies, *Business—a Profession*, Boston, Small Maynard and Company, 1914.
2. Abraham Flexner, Is Social Work a Profession ? *School and Society*, 20 June, 1915, P. 901;

   Dale Yoder, *Personnel Principles and Policies*, Englewood Cliffs, New Jersy, Prentice Hall Inc., 1952, pp. 45–46;

   Morris L. Cogan, *Harvard Educational Review*, 1953;

   H. L. Wilensky, The Professionalisation of Every one ?' *American Journal of Sociology*, 6 September, 1954;

   Ernest Greenwood, Attributes of a Profession, *Social Work*, Vol.2, July, 1957, pp. 45–55;

   E.F.L. Breach, (Ed.), *The Principles and Practices of Management*, London,

Longmans, Green & Company Ltd., 1963, p. 1035;

G. Millerson, *The Qualifying Associations*, London, Routledge and Kegan Paul, 1964;

Howard M. Vollmer and Donald L. Mills (Eds.), *Professionalisation*, Englewood Cliffs, New Jersy, Prentice Hall Inc., 1966, pp. 43–44;

Robert H. Roy and James H. MacNeill, *Horizons for a Profession*, New York, American Institute of Certified Public Accounts., 1967;

Bernard Barbar, "Is American Business Becoming Professionalised?" in Edward A. Tiryakien, (Ed.), *Sociological Theory*, New York, Harper & Row, 1967, pp. 121–145;

George Strauss and Leonard R. Sayles, *Personnel the Human Problems of Management*, New Delhi, Prentice Hall of India Pvt. Ltd., 1968, p. 70;

Dalton E. McFarland, *Personnel Management Theory and Practice*, London, McMillan Company Ltd., 1968;

K.R. Andrews, "Toward Professionalisation in Business Management", *Harvard Business Review*, March–April, 1969, pp. 40–60;

Wilbert E. Scheer, *Personnel Directors' Hand Book*, Chicago, The Dartnell Corporation, 1970, P. 906;

Prakash Tandon, *Professional Management in India—its Potential and Problems*, Ludhiana, Punjab Agricultural University Press, 1974;

S.P. Sharma, *Professional Management in India*, New Delhi, Deep and Deep Publications, 1982;

F.E. Kast & James E. Rosenzweig, *Organisation and Management—A Systems and Contingency Approach*, New York, McGraw Hill Book Company, Inc., 1985, pp. 173–174.

3. Alexander Morris Carr-Saunders and P.A. Wilson, *The Professions*, Oxford, Clarindon Press, 1933.

4. A. W. Gouldner, "Cosmopolitan and Locals : Towards an Analysis of Latent Social Roles–I" *Administrative Science Quarterly*, Vol. 2, 1957-58, pp. 281-306.

5. E.B. Flippo, *Principles of Personnel Management*, Tokyo, McGraw Hill Kogakusha, 1976. pp. 11–12.

6. Peter F. Drucker, *The Practice of Management*, London, Mercury Books, 1961, p. 368.

7. Shaun Tyson and Allan Fell, *Evaluating the Personnel Function*, London,

Hutchinson Personnel Management Services, 1986, p.53.

8. Elite is defined as "a minority group (or category) of individuals within a society, who may be socially acknowledged as superior in some sense and who influence or control some or all of the other segments of the society". Duncan Mitchell (Ed.), *A Dictionary of Sociology*, London, Routledge & Kegan Paul, 1968, p. 64.
9. T.B. Bottomore, *Elites and Society*, 1964.
10. Claude S. George (Jr.), *The History of Management Thought*, New Delhi, Prentice Hall of India Pvt. Ltd., 1974, pp. 38–39.
11. George (Jr.), *The History*, pp. 50–59.
12. George (Jr.), *The History*, pp. 59–62.
13. Cyril Curtis Ling, *The Management of Personnel Relations : History and Origins*, Richard D. Irwin, Illinois, 1965, pp. 71–76.
14. The six factors which stimulated the welfare movement were (i) erosion of the employer-employee relationship; (ii) evil influences of factory system on workers; (iii) labour strife of the post civil war period; (iv) lack of essential community facilities; (v) positive attitude of the employers towards benefit of welfare work; and (vi) desire to thwart unions. Ling, *The Management*, p. 81.
15. Oscar W. Nester, *A History of Personnel Administration 1890–1910*, Ph.D. Dissertation, University of Pennsylvania, 1954; Louis A. Boettinger, *Employee Welfare Work*, New York, Ronald Press Co., 1923.
16. Henry Eilbirt, "The Development of Personnel Management in United States, *Business History Review*, Vol. 33 (Autumn, 1959), pp. 345–65.
17. Eilbirt, *Business*, pp. 345–65.
18. Gertrude Beeks, "The New Profession, *National Civic Federation Review*, Vol. 1 (Feb. 1, 1905), p. 12.
19. Eilbirt, *Business*, p. 350.
20. Ordway Tead, "Personnel Administration", *Encyclopaedia of Social Sciences*, Vol. 12, 1934, p. 88.
21. F.W. Taylor, *Principles of Scientific Management*, New York, Harper and Brothers, 1911.
22. Apart from recognising planning activity in management, Babbage also discussed several motivational tools like incentive systems, profit sharing schemes and plans allowing employees to participate in establishing shop rules. See Charles Babbage, *On the Economy of Machinery and Manufac-*

turers, London, Charles Knight, 1832.

23. Andrew Ure in his moral system recognised some possible motivating tools such as price rates, safety and health provisions and recreation plans. See Andrew Ure, *The Philosophy of Manufacturers*, London, Charles Knight, 1835.

24. Ling, *The Management*, pp. 366–367.

25. Nick Cowan, "Change and the Personnel Profession", *Personnel Management*, January, 1988, p. 36.

26. The Americal Management Association which started in 1923 and the British Institute of Management that started in 1947 testify this contention.

27. For details see Long, *The Management*, pp. 376–400.

28. The publication of "Personnel during the First World War, which brought about articles dating back to last decade of 19th Century, marked the beginning of professional journal; while the book launched by Tead and Metcalf in 1920 with the title "Personnel Administration was followed by many more publications in later years. Ling, *The Management*, 400–401.

29. Gertrude Beeks (1905) and Meyer Bloomfield (1915) termed it as a new profession.

30. Bloomfield by 1919 also had called it a new profession. See Ling, *The Management*, p. 516.

31. Carr-Saunders and Wilson, *The Professions*, 1933.

32. Samuel L.H. Burk, "The Personnel Profession—Its Present and Future Status", *Personnel Organisation and Personnel Development, Personnel Series*, No. 14, New York, American Management Association, 1943, pp. 40–47.

33. Dale Yoder, "Trends towards professionalisation in Personnel Work", *Personnel Journal*, Vol. 28, No. 9, February, 1950, pp. 326–329.

34. Peter F. Drucker, "Personnel Management—Its Assets and Liabilities", *Dun's Review and Modern Industry*, Vol. 63, No. 2314. (June, 1954), pp. 42–43, 80–94.

35. Lawrance A. Appley, "Personnel Administration at Mid-Century", in *Management in Action*, Bombay, The Times of India, Press, 1965, pp. 373–382.

36. Dale Yoder, H.G. Heneman (Jr.), John G. Turnbell, C. Hrold Stone, *Handbook of Personnel Management and Labour Relations*, New York, McGraw Hill Book Co. Inc., 1958, pp. 24–25.

37. Frank B. Miller, "Why I am for professionalising ?" *Personnel Journal*, Vol. 38, No. 3, July–August, 1959, p. 91.
38. Frank B. Miller, The Personnel Dilemma : Profession or not ? *Personnel Journal*, Vol. 38, No. 2, June 1959, p. 55.
39. Ewing W. Reilley, "The Opportunity and the Challenge of Personnel Administration in Robert E. Finley, (Ed.) *The Personnel Man and his Job*, Bombay, D.B. Taraporevala Co. Pvt. Ltd., 1962, pp. 12–22.
40. S. Vincent Wilking, "The Status of Today's Personnel Man", in Finley (Ed.), *The Personnel*, pp. 25–27.
41. Ling, *The Management*, P. 497.
42. Dale S. Beach, *Personnel—The Management of People at Work*, New York, Mac Millan Co., 1965, p. 817.
43. Dalton E. McFarland, *Personnel Management : Theory and Practice,* London, The Mac Millan Company, 1968, P. 112.
44. Wendell French, *The Personnel Management Processes*, Boston, Houghton Mifflin Co., 1970, p. 605.
45. George Ritzer and Harrison M. Trice, "An Occupation in Conflict : A Study of the Personnel Manager", New York State School of Industrial and Labour Relations, Cornell University, 1969.
46. George Ritzer, "The Professionals : Will Personnel Occupations, Ever Become Professions ?" *The Personnel Administration*, Vol. 16: 3, 1971, pp. 34–36.
47. Herbert E. Meyers, cited in the Text.
48. John B. Miner, "Levels of Motivation to Manage among Personnel and Industrial Relations Managers", *Journal of Applied Psychology*, Vol. 61, No. 4, 1976, pp. 419–427.
49. Erwin S. Stanton, "Last Chance for Personnel to come of Age", *The Personnel Administrator*, Vol. 20, No. 7 (1975), pp. 14–16, 49.
50. John B. Miner and Mary Green Miner, *Personnel and Industrial Relations—A Managerial Approach*, New York, Mac Millan Publishing Co., Inc., 1973, pp. 586–588.
51. G. Hunter, *The Role of Personnel Officer*, London, Institute of Personnel Management, 1957.
52. T.J. Watson, *The Personnel Managers*, London, Routledge and Kegan Paul, 1977.
53. K. Legge, *Power, Innovation and Problem Solving in Personnel Manage-*

ment, London, McGraw Hill, 1978.

54. S. Tyson, "*Specialists in Ambiguity : Personnel Management as an Occupation*", Ph.D. Thesis, London University, 1979.

55. J. Henstridge, "Personnel Management—A Framework for Analysis", *Personnel Review*, Vol. 4, No. 1, 1975, p. 51.

56. K. Manning, "The Rise and Fall of Personnel", *Management Today*, March, 1983, p. 74.

57. P. Copping and C. Pickles, "Who goes into Personnel ?" *Personnel Executive*, October, 1981, p. 31.

58. K. Legge and M. Exley, "Authority Ambiguity and Adaptation : The Personnel Specialists Dilemma", *Industrial Relations Journal*, Vol. 6, No. 3, 1975, pp. 51–65.

59. Watson, *The Personnel.*

60. K. Thurley, "Personnel Management in U.K.—A Case for Urgent Treatment"? *Personnel Management* (August, 1981), p. 28.

61. IIPM, *Personnel Management in India : The Practical Approach to Human Relations in Industry*, Bombay, Asia Publishing House, 1973; J.A. Panakal, et al, (Eds.), *Readings in Personnel Management*, Calcutta, Orient Longmans, 1973.

62. M.N. Rudrabasava Raj, Personnel Administration in India, Poona, Vaikuntha Mehta National Institute of Co-operative Management, 1969; L. Prasad, Personnel Management and Industrial Relations, Bombay, Progressive Co-operation Pvt. Ltd., 1973; G.C., Patro, Human Resources Management, Delhi, Discovery Publishing House, 1989; A.K. Mohapatra and G.C. Patro, Managing Manpower at work, New Delhi, Discovery Publishing House, 1989.

63. S.K. Roy and A.S.K. Menon, Motivation and Organisational Effectiveness, New Delhi, Sri Ram Centre for Industrial Relation and Human Resources, 1974; S.D. Kapoor, "The Extent of job satisfaction among Indian Industrial Workers—A Normative Study". Journal of Indian Academy of Applied Psychology, 1968, Vol. 5, No. 1, pp. 13–19.

64. K.N. Vaid, The Labour Welfare Officer, Delhi, Delhi School of Social Work, 1962.

65. National Institute of Labour Management, A Study of Personnel Officers in Greater Bombay, Bombay, The Author, 1966.

66. K.C. Alexander, Reorient Personnel Management, *Integrated Management*,

May, 1969, pp. 45–52.

67. R.S. Kamat, How Personnel Management can be made more dynamic, *Capital*, November, 12, 1970, pp. 823–824.

68. C.S. Myers and S., Kanappan, *Labour Management Relations in India*, Bombay, Asia Publishing House, 1970.

69. R.S. Tarneja, *Personnel Managers at Work*, Madras, Human Resources Foundation, 1968; R.P. Billimoria, "The Future Role of Personnel Officers", in J.A. Panakal, et al, (Eds.), *Readings in.*

70. K.K. Jacob, *Personnel Management in India—A Study of Training and Functions of Personnel Officers*, Udaipur, S.J.C. Publications, 1973; K.B. Akhilesh and R. Sekar, Personnel Profession in India : Selected Results of a National Survey in K.B.

71. Akhilesh and D.R. Nagaraj (Eds.), *Human Resources Management—2000: Indian Perspectives*, New Delhi, NIPM, Wiley Eastern Limited, 1990, pp. 17–31.

72. The justification and purpose of the questionnair and the sampling design are discussed in Chapter IV.

2

Genesis of Personnel Profession in India (Upto 1947)

Introduction

Personnel Management is a post-industrial development in any country. Taking cue from a more or less uniform global pattern, this chapter attempts to highlight the genesis of personnel profession in India. It is proposed to cover the history upto 1947, the year of Indian independence. The post-independence period is always accredited as the beginning of a new era in terms of a definite industrial policy, planned economic development, clear-cut Government labour policies. So, this phase is discussed in the next chapter reflecting the current stature of personnel profession in India.

Industrialization in India

India had a flourishing cottage industry prior to large scale industrialization which began in a modest way after mid 19th century[1]. The British policy of exploiting the Indian market with British goods produced in Great Britain from the raw materials procured from India, was responsible for the decay in the cottage industry. However, the British entrepreneurs after 1850 provided leadership in developing mining, plantation and some organised manufacturing industries like cotton textile, jute and tanneries, besides developing the railways as an important infrastructure for industrialization. The initial pace of industrialization was painfully slow, partly because of the British Government's Laissez Faire policy and partly due to the non-availability of requisite skill, capital and entrepreneurship from among the Indians. It was only after 1875 that the factory system began to progress and by the first decade of the present century along with steel mills, many mineral industries and small miscellaneous industries were set up. It was in the inter-war period that there was a bloom[2] in the growth of industries. The second World War provided a stimulus to Indian industries to meet the war needs, as a result of which small scale industries expanded and many new industries were started. The growth in the industrialization can be gauged form the fact that from 565 factories in 1892 it had gone upto 14, 576 by the year 1947. (Table 2.1)

Development of Personnel Functionaries

The consequences of industrialization such as the emergence of industrial work-force, trade unionism and labour legislation are contributory to the emergence of personnel management. The evils of industrialization like unhygienic working conditions, exploitation of workers strengthened the industrial welfare movement thereby leading to further consolidation of personnel management. Presently, it is attempted here to highlight the contributions made by the industrial labour force, trade unionism, welfare movement and labour legislation towards development of personnel management in India.

Emergence and Characteristics of Indian Industrial Work-force

With the expansion of industrialization, more specifically, the transport industry (railways), mines, plantations and manufacturing industries, there was a concomitant rise in the industrial Work-force in India. While data pertaining to other sectors are not available, the number of factories and workers employed from 1892 to 1947 as depicted in Table 2.1 is indicative of a general growth of industrial Work-force.

The growth of modern industries demanded employment of labour in large numbers. This led to large scale migration of people from the rural pockets to the up-coming industrial urban centres. These early migrants

Table 2.1 : Number of Factories and Workers employed from 1892 to 1947

Year	*No. of Factories*	*No. of Workers employed*
1892	656	316816
1894	815	349810
1902	1533	541634
1912	2710	869643
1914	2936	950973
1918	3436	1122922
1923	5985	1409137
1929	7153	1455092
1933	8542	1403212
1939	10466	1751137
1943	13209	2436312
1944	14071	2522753
1945	14761	2647949
1946	14205	2314587
1947	14576	2274689

Source: Government of India, *Report of the Labour Investigation Committee*. 1944, P. 12; C.B. Memoria, *Labour Problems and Social Welfare in India*, Allahabad, Kitab Mahal, 1966, pp. 9, 10; R.C. Saxena, *Labour Problems and Social Welfare*, Meerut, K. Nath & Co., 1986, p.9.

who came from the traditional village societies based on hierarchy of caste were socially and economically disabled groups, namely, the agricultural workers and the artisans. The agricultural labourers migrated because of the pressure of population on land while the cause of migration of the artisans was the decay in the cottage industries. These migrants sought employment in textiles, tanneries, railway workshops and other urban industries.

A great majority of the early industrial labour force at heart were villagers as they were born and brought up in the villages. They had village traditions and had retained their village connections for several reasons. Firstly, they were not prompted by the lure of the city life or by any great ambition. Secondly, opportunities for employment of women and children in towns being relatively scarce, the workers were forced to leave their families in the native settings. As a result the worker had to lead virtually an isolated life in the milieu of strange traditions. Further, the memories of his native place and lack of ability to establish a permanent home in the urban centres created a desire for returning to the villages frequently. These dynamics are popularly known as the push and pull factor and village nexus[3]. Because of absence of a permanent attachment to the industries, the industrial workers had no commitment to the industrial way of life[4]. However, by 1946, as per the report of the Rege Committee[5], the working-class had become stabilised and their ties with villages loosened. This indicates the improved commitment[6] to the industrial way of life[7].

One of the characteristics of labour market during the early period of industrialization was the short supply of labour. The reason was that, they were reluctant to move out of their villages and work in distant places under strange environment. The situation improved by 1875[8] and greater number of workers migrated to the industrial centres. Yet, the quality of labour supply was so poor that, the requisite skill to cope with the technology was not available[9]. The absenteeism and labour turnover were so high that a steady supply of labour was the primary need of industries. In the 'Jobber' system the British employers found a solution to the aforesaid problems afflicting the labour market. The primary function of the Jobber was to act as a middleman to hire the labour on behalf of the employers. They were to ensure the attendance of the labour, provide initial training to the labour and above all to oversee their performance. With a workable knowledge of English, the Jobbers used to act as interpreters for the Englishmen technicians. They played such a pivotal role in the then industries that they virtually substituted supervisors and middle managers. Though, this system was quite handy for the British employers, it turned out to be an institution of exploitation for the workers. The Jobbers though paid by the employers on account of their power to grant or withhold employment to the job seekers could exploit the workers by demanding and obtaining 'Baksheesh' or 'Dasturi' (fee, commission or bride)[10].

The evils of the Jobber System, was severely criticized by the Royal

Commission on Labour which issued a scathing denunciation of the system and recommended that each mill should appoint a labour officer who would be responsible for all hiring[11]. The commission prescribed integrity, personality, energy, the gift of understanding individuals and linguistic facility as the main qualities of the labour officers[12]. After initial resentment the Bombay Mill Owners' Association recommended its members to appoint labour officers. By 1938, some organizations had employed labour officers to look after hiring. These characteristics of labour and the system of Jobber paved the path for organising a very important personnel function, namely recruitment.

Early Trade Unionism

Another contemporaneous development, the trade union movement which began in the last decade of the 19th century but formalised only in the second decade of the present century, was a contributory for the emergence of personnel management in India. Indian Trade Union Movement as elsewhere was also a post industrial development. But in comparison to the West the Trade Union movement in India was considerably delayed[13].

Another specific feature of the Indian labour movement is that, to a great extent it has remained confined only to the organised sector of the economy. And incidentally it is the organised industries in which the personnel management marked a beginning.

The Indian labour movement started from 1875 on an extremely moderate and cautious way making use of institutions of the democratic rights and liberties, memorials and petitions. Some philanthropists and social workers like S.S. Bangalee, L.M. Lokhande and others started an agitation to draw the attention of the government to the deplorable conditions of the workers at the time the first Factories Commission was appointed in 1875. In later years many organizations like the Mill Hands Association (1890), the Amalgamated Society of Railway Servants of India and Burma (1897), Printers Union, Calcutta (1905), Bombay Postal Union (1907), the Kamagarh Hitvardhak Sabha (1910) were formed. These organizations though worked for labour[14] but could not claim the status of trade unions and many of them became defunct soon after their formation.

Thus it is evident that even after more than half a century after industrialization began in India, Trade Union movement remained still in a dormant stage. This was because of the court injunctions against strike and the prosecution of trade unionists under the doctrines of criminal conspiracy and restraint of trade and breach of contract under the common law which led the prosecution of B.P. Wadia, the president of Madras Labour Union[15] in 1920.

The prosecution of B.P. Wadia not only opened the eyes of the trade unionists but also created consciousness among the public, politicians and industrial workers of both U.K. and India. As a result the Indian Trade Union Act, 1926 was enacted which legalised the formation of trade unions, provided immunization against criminal liability and provided security against cases of civil damages arising out of trade disputes.

Another development which was instrumental in the emergence of the trade union movement was the formation of the International Labour Organisation (ILO) in 1919, with India as a founding member. In order to send the workers' representatives to the ILO the All India Trade Union Congress, the first national centre of workers, was formed in 1920. After the formalisation the trade unions became a force in the National Movement. The post First World War period witnessed a spate of strikes and work stoppages which can be attributed to the emergence and growth of trade unions as well as to the war time trails and tribulations of the working class. During the period 1927 and 1947 the number of unions increased from 29 to 1833, while the membership increased from 101 thousand to 1331 thousand[16]. Further these trade union spearheaded many strikes and other work stoppages. The work stoppages and lock-outs together accounted for around 16.5 million mandays lost in 1947 as against 7 million mandays lost in 1921[17]. Thus, trade unionism along with its own growth also enhanced the number of industrial disputes.

A need arose on the part of the employers to deal with the trade unions which received legal status after the Trade Unions Act of 1926. To start with, attempts were made by the employers to curb trade unionism. For this purpose the organisations employed retired police and military personnel ostensibly to deal with the disturbances caused by the trade unions. The Government did not play much of an active role excepting enactment of law to regulate labour-management relations. Trade unionism necessitated negotiations and administration of agreements which paved the path for the emergence of industrial relations functions in the Indian industries.

Welfare Movement

Industrialization, while contributed for economic prosperity, was also responsible for creating a number of labour problems like bad working conditions, long hours of work, low wages, exploitation of women and children, over crowding etc. Also health, medical, safety provisions were conspicuous by their absence. These conditions prompted the attention of philanthropists and social workers and social agencies who organised welfare programmes like education, medical, etc. on a nominal basis. It was during and the post First World War period the employers initiated welfare programmes on their own. The programmes initiated by them were worker's education, sanitation, medical relief including maternity, child care and development of habits of thrift, savings and abstinancy from drinking. Some mills like Empress Mills, (Nagpur); TISCO, (Jameshedpur), etc. also appointed Welfare Officers[18]. The inter-war period witnessed certain developments which provided a momentum to the labour welfare movement in India. The formation of ILO in 1919 which through its conventions and recommendations could influence the introduction of many welfare provisions in India. Another landmark in the filed of labour welfare during this period was the appointment of Royal Commission of Labour in 1929 which investigated into the working conditions in different industries and suggested different welfare measures. The formation of popular Congress governments in late 1930s in different provinces raised hopes among the workers for improvement of their conditions. The provincial Governments appointed Labour Investigation Committees to enquire into and improvise the conditions of labour.

The Second World War provided a further impetus to the welfare movement. In order to maintain uninterrupted production as well as to improve efficiency of the workers many employers initiated different welfare programmes. The Government also launched schemes of welfare in its ordinance and ammunition factories to keep morale and boost war production. Many of these welfare programmes were continued even after the Second World War. The Labour Investigations Committee appointed by the Government in mid-1940s recommended to bring out improvement in working conditions, health, welfare and safety.

The employers' intentions in providing welfare measures were not accepted because of two coequal apprehensions, namely, (1) welfare smacked to paternalism[19]. (2) welfare work may interfere with legitimate growth of trade unionism[20]. During and after Second World War, the recognition given to welfare as an efficiency boosting measure was responsible for making labour welfare an important part of personnel function.

Growth of Labour Legislation

The growth of labour legislation had also contributed to the development of personnel management in India. The earliest labour legislations those prevalent were, the Apprentices Act, 1850; the Fatal Accident Act, 1853; Merchant Shipping Act, 1859. These acts were mostly meant for regulating employment rather than improving the conditions of labour. The first legislation which provided some relief in terms of employment of women and children, weekly holiday and safety was the Factories Act of 1881. The Act was subsequently amended in 1891, 1911, 1922, 1934 expanding its scope and improving the legislative standards relating to conditions and hours of work. The 1920s saw the enactment of the Workmen's Compensation Act, 1923 and the Trade Union Act, 1926. The Trade Disputes Act which was enacted in 1929 on an experimental basis was put on the statute book permanently in 1934. The Payment of Wages Act was enacted in 1936 to regulate the timely payment of wages and restriction on deduction.

The growth of the legislation and the compliance requirements and the administrative pressures which increased with the formation of popular Congress Governments in most provinces in late 1930s forced to employ full-time labour officers and/or labour lawyers[21].

Rule 81 A which was added to the Defence of India Rules in 1942 empowered the Government to prohibit strikes and lockouts; to refer any dispute to conciliation and adjudication; to require employers to observe specific terms and conditions and to enforce the decisions of the adjudicators. The enactment of the Industrial Employment (Standing Orders) Act, 1946 required the employers to formally define conditions of employment under them.

It can be observed from the growth of the labour legislation that, all the three core functional areas, namely, labour welfare, industrial relations and personnel administration find their roots in the genesis of different laws. No other development like welfare movement, trade unionism, Jobbers system vis-a-vis labour officer could make a wholesome contribution to the personnel management as labour legislation. In one way labour legislation transcends all the developments.

Tying the Loose Ends of the Genesis

The discussions made above reveal that four contemporaneous and mutually complementary developments in the post industrialization period in India are responsible for the development of labour functionaries in Industrial Organizations. They are (1) migratory characteristics of labour, (2) Trade Union movement, (3) welfare movement, and (4) labour legislation. The welfare workers/ secretaries, the police and military personnel, the labour officers may be regarded as the precursors of modern personnel officers. But they cannot be accredited as professionals. The rationale of this observation can be appreciated in the light of the discussions made below.

Growth of Personnel Management As A Discipline

There was no formal training[22] for labour welfare as a profession before the establishment of the Dorabji Tata Graduate School of Social Work in Bombay in 1936[23]. The Mill Owners' Association in Bombay and Ahmedabad as well as the Indian Jute Mills Association at Calcutta had pioneered in-service training of short duration for working labour officers in cotton and jute industries respectively. The initial efforts of the Tata School was to train the professional Social Workers against the long and rich tradition of voluntary social service in the country. The training imparted was of generic nature, wherein the trainees were trained to apply case work, group work and community organisation techniques to deal with individual, group and community problems of workers in industry respectively. However, the thrust of traditional American Social Work

Practices which reeled round family case work, psychiatric and medical social work could be of little use in-industrial setting. Thus the efforts of the Tata School though was the first of its kind in the country was not adequate to provide a discipline base to personnel management.

The in-service training programmes organised by the Indian Jute Mills Association (IJMA) culminated in the establishment of the Indian Institute of Social Welfare and Business Management at Calcutta in the year 1942. Initially the thrust of training programmes given by this institute was on social work coupled with knowledge in existing labour legislations. Thus the development of the discipline base in personnel management till 1947 was not contributory for satisfying any claims of professionalization.

Growth of Management as a Profession in India

British and European Companies in India, who adopted the managing agency system in the initial stages got their managers i.e., covenanted officers[24] on contract from their respective countries. The Indian companies mostly assigned the management position to their own family members. But none of them had any formal training in management. In mid-thirties the British companies started taking the young Indian graduates from Oxford and Cambridge, well connected, as a concession to influence and growing aspirations. In 1937 there were about 25 young Indian professional managers in international companies. In Indian family companies there were very few truly professional managers[25]. For general management they mostly relied upon their family members and when they ran out of them, men of their caste and religion filled in the posts. This led to a nepotistic patrimonial management system devoid of professionalism.

Another development in the year 1860, when the first Indian joined the Indian Civil service marked the beginning of the emergence of bureaucratic administration. However, it was during the Second World War, that British managers were called off and as their members depleted, more and more Indians, some from the Indian Civil Service were taken as managers in industries[26]. It was then the professional management in India made a beginning.

In this perspective of general management making a modest beginning as a profession by the end of Second World War when we observe that, personnel management was yet to take steps towards professionalism by 1947 is quite natural. Because personnel management obviously is a part of general management.

REFERENCES

1. Industrialization in India emerged around a century later than that of U.K. and other Western Countries.
2. S.D. Punekar, S.B. Deodhar and S. Sankaran, *Labour Welfare, Trade Unionism and Industrial Relation*, Bombay, Himalaya Publishing House, 1981, p.14.
3. Richard D. Lambert, *Workers, Factories and Social Change in India*, Bombay, Asia Publishing House, 1963, pp. 79-81.
4. Government of India, *Report of Royal Commission on Labour in India, 1931*, New Delhi, Agricole Publishing Academy, 1983, (Reprint).
5. Report of the Labour Investigation Committee, 1944, p.68.
6. Charles A. Myers observes that "a committed industrial labour can be said to have developed when workers no longer look on their industrial employment as temporary". *Labour Problems in the Industrialization of India*, Cambridge, Mass: Harvard University Press, 1958, p. 36.
7. Moore & Feldman observe that, "commitment involves both performance and acceptance of the behaviours appropriate to an industrial way of life". For details refer W.E. Moore and A.S. Feldman (Eds.), *Labour Commitment and Social Change in Developing Societies*, New York, Social Science Research Council, 1960, p.1.
8. A Mill Manager Mr. Bowler testified before the Factory Commission in 1875 that there was no difficult in supply of labour to the mills in Bombay, *Report of the Factory Commission*, 1875, p.75.
9. Morris D. Morris, *The Emergence of an Industrial Labour Force in India: A study of the Bombay Cotton Mills, (1854-1947)*, Bombay, Oxford University Press, 1965, p. 52.
10. Morris, *Emergence*, p.134.
11. Government of India, *The Royal Commission*, p. 24. (However, there is evidence of the Tata Iron & Steel Company at Jamshedpur creating a welfare

department in 1917 and appointing welfare officers in 1923).

12. Government, *Royal commission*, P.25.

13. G.P. Sinha and P.R.N. Sinha, *Industrial Relations and Labour Legislation*, New Delhi, Oxford and IBH Publishing Co., 1977, p.88.

14. Oscar A. Ornati rightly observed that "born out of philanthropy, it was a movement for the worker rather than by the worker". *Jobs and Workers in India*, Ithaca, Cornell University, 1955, p. 98.

15. Madras Labour Union formed in 1918 is considered to be the Industrial Trade Union, when it resorted to strike the employers not only could bring injunctions against strike but also prosecuted B.P. Wadia.

16. For details see G.K. Sharma, *Labour Movement in India—Its past and present*, New Delhi, Sterling Publishers Pvt. Ltd., 1971, Table. 4, p. 176; Sinha and Sinha, *Industrial*, Tables, 6&7, pp. 107 and 110.

17. For details see, Sinha and Sinha, *Industrial*, Tables, 5& 8, p. 103,111.

18. Government, *Royal Commission*, pp. 258-260.

19. Gopal C. Rath, *The Welfare Officer in Indian Industry*, M.S. Dissertation, Cornell University (Unpublished), 1956, p. 14.

20. This contention was disputed by the All India Industrial Welfare Conference held in 1922 which urged the employers and the advocates of trade unionism recognised the desirability of welfare work both on humanitarian and efficiency ground, 11 PM, *Personnel management in India: The Practical Approach to Human Relations in Industry*, Bombay, Asia Publishing House, 1973, p. 42.

21. L.S. Kudchedkar, *Aspects of Personnel Management and Industrial Relations*, New Delhi, Tata McGraw Hill Publishing Co. Ltd., 1979, p.54.

22. The need for formal training perhaps was not realised because, even the RCL observed that "special technical qualifications are not essential for the labour officers, though general knowledge... integrity, personality, energy, the gift of understanding individuals and the linguistic facility are the main qualities required'. Needless to reiterate that these are mostly qualities but not qualifications. Government, *Royal Commission*, p. 25.

23. It came to be known as Tata Institute of Social Sciences since 1944.

24. N.N. Chatterjee, *Management of Personnel in Indian Enterprises*, Calcutta, Allied Book Agency, 1978, p.3.

25. Prakash Tandon, *Professional Management in India; Its Potential and Problems*, Ludhiana, Punjab Agricultural University, 1974, p. 8-9.

26. Tandon, *Professional*, p.9.

3

Current Status of Personnel Profession in India : Historical Facts

Introduction

The developments and efforts in the pre-independence India with regard to the origin and growth of personnel profession indicated that, this period witnessed a modest yet important beginning towards professionalisation. In order to sketch out the present status of the personnel profession, the post-independence period developments and efforts need to be highlighted in all those areas covered in the previous chapter. This chapter, thus depicts the current status of personnel profession in India with the help of historical facts.

Industrialization

The post-independence period in India witnessed an era of intensive industrial development. However, in the initial years following independence, industrialization was restricted because of economic uncertainties, non-availability of machinery and technical know-how, shortage of raw material and above all frequent disputes between labour and capital. Under these circumstances the Tripartite Industries Conference called in December, 1947, adopted a three year Truce Resolution between labour and capital. The Government also provided certain incentives, established the Industrial Finance Corporation and laid down a definite Industrial Policy. The Industrial Policy Resolution of 1948 gave expression to the system of Mixed Economy by involving both Government and Private enterprises in launching industries.

Following independence, India launched the process of planning for growth with the formation of the First Five Year Plan in 1950-51. Since then the country has made considerable progress in almost all sectors of the economy. In the process of planned development, industrialization only got a momentum since the launching of the Second Five Year Plan in a 1955-56. During the same period the government declared its new Industrial Policy by revising its earlier policy laid dawn in 1948. As a result, there was considerable expansion of the industrial sector leading to a higher rate of industrial production.

The annual rate of growth of industrial production during 1951-86 (refer Table 3.1) at 5.7 per cent though appears to be modest; yet was considerably higher than the growth rate of 2 per cent marked during the first half of the 20th century. Since 1951, the decade wise growth rate was the highest during 1951-60 at 6.1 per cent. Thereafter it declined to 5.3 per cent during 1960-70 and further to 4.2 per cent during 1970-80. The period 1981-82 to 1988-89 however witnessed in increase in the industrial production which stood at 7.7 per cent on an average (Table 3.2). The rate of industrial growth which was 8.7 per cent in April 1989 has declined to 5.7 per cent in December, 1989[1]. Considering the plan period analysis, the annual average growth rate was the highest at 9 per cent during 1961-65 and lowest at 3.3 per cent during the next 5 years i.e., 1966-70. It can also be observed that the annual growth rate picked up significantly to 4.9 per cent during 1976-80 and further to 6.5 per cent during 1981-85. The highest industrial growth rate i.e. 11 per cent during any years since 1951 was noted in 1976.

Since 1951 the rate of growth of industrial production as is evident from the above discussions can be said to be satisfactory. This is also proved when we take into account the contribution of industrial sector to the economy. The share of the mining, manufacturing and construction which was 14.9 per cent in 1950-51 increased to 22 per cent in 1965-66.

Table 3.1 : Index of Industrial Production during 1951–86 (Base 1970=100)

Year	*Index of Production*	*Percent of change*	*Year*	*Index of Production*	*Percent of change*
1951	32.6	--	1972	110.6	5.9
1955	39.9	5.2	1973	111.1	0.5
1956	43.2	8.3	1974	113.1	1.8
1960	55.5	6.5	1975	119.2	5.4
1961	60.6	9.2	1976	132.3	11.0
1962	66.4	9.6	1977	138.4	4.6
1963	71.9	8.3	1978	148.7	7.4
1964	78.1	8.6	1979	149.6	0.6
1965	85.3	9.2	1980	150.7	0.7
1966	85.0	–0.4	1981	164.7	9.3
1967	83.9	–1.3	1982	172.1	4.5
1968	89.4	6.6	1983	181.2	5.3
1969	95.7	6.4	1984	194.2	7.2
1970	100.0	5.2	1985	206.2	6.2
1971	104.4	4.4	1986	220.6	7.0

Source : P.R. Brahmananda and V.R. Panchmukhi (eds), The Development Process of Indian Economy, Bombay, Himalaya Publishing House, 1987, p. 303.

Table 3.2 : Index of Industrial Production since 1980–81 to 1988–89 (Base 1980–81 =100)

Year	*Index of Production*	*Percent of Change*
1980–81	100	--
1981–82	109.3	9.3
1982–83	112.8	3.2
1983–84	120.4	6.7
1984–85	130.7	8.6
1985–86	142.1	8.7
1986–87	155.1	9.1
1987–88	166.4	7.3
1988–89	181.1	8.8
Average		7.7

Source : Government of India, Economic Survey, 1988–89, New Delhi, Ministry of Finance, 1990, p. S36.

Thereafter, however, its share was marginally lower at 21.6 per cent in 1984-85.

Industrial Workforce in Independent India

The growth rate in industrialization concomitantly resulted in increase in the number of industrial workforce. The trend shows that the employment in the organized sector[2] has improved over the years 1955-66 to 1987-88 (see Table 3.3).

The employment in the organized sector has registered as 2.5 times increase in the year 1987-88 over the year 1955-56. Expectedly the public sector has generated more employment than the private sector.

Table 3.3 : Employment in Organised Sector during 1955–56 to 1987–88 (in lakhs)

Year	*Employment in Public Sector*	*Employment in Private Sector*	*Total*
1955–56	52.34	50.40	102.74
1960–61	70.50	50.40	120.90
1965–66	93.78	68.10	161.88
1970–71	107.31	67.60	174.91
1975–76	133.22	68.44	201.66
1976–77	137.66	68.67	206.33
1977–78	142.00	70.43	212.43
1978–79	146.76	72.08	218.84
1979–80	150.78	72.27	223.05
1980–81	154.84	73.95	228.79
1981–82	159.46	75.47	234.93
1982–83	164.56	75.52	240.08
1983–84	168.69	73.45	242.14
1984–85	172.69	73.09	245.78
1985–86	176.83	73.73	250.56
1986–87	180.25	73.64	253.89
1987–88	183.20 (P)	73.91 (P)	257.11

P = Provisional

Source : Brahmananda and Panchmukhi, The Development, p. 1218; Government, Economic Survey, p. S47 and S48.

Besides the expansion of the organized sectors, the factory sector expanded both in terms of number of factories and average employment since 1948 (Table 3.4).

The table indicates that there is a ten fold increase in the number of working factories over the period from 1948 to 1985. The average daily employment on the other hand has made a 3.2 fold increase. This is indicative of the trend that the number of small factories having low employment potential has increased over years. This trend is further substantiated by the fact that the average employment per factory has decreased to 42 in 1985 from 148 in the year 1948.

Table 3.4 : Number of Working Factories and Average of Daily Employment

Year	*No. of working factories*	*No. of daily employment*
1948	15,906	23,60,201
1949	19,829	24,33,966
1950	27,754	25,04,399
1951	30,836	25,36,544
1952	30,351	25,67,453
1953	30,450	25,28,026
1954	30,053	25,83,757
1956	37,162	34,01,599
1957	37,896	33,66,247
1958	41,542	34,12,985
1961	50,095	39,18,000
1966	64,872	47,02,000
1967	67,582	47,60,000
1968	68,544	47,56,000
1969	71,673	47,71,000
1975	1,03,795	57,72,000
1979	1,35,330	68,01,544
1980	1,40,843	70,03,596
1981	1,49,285	73,14,965
1985	1,80,572	75,84,024

Source : Compiled from Secondary Sources.

Reflecting on the level of skill development among the work force in the country, it can be observed that in comparison to the period preceding the independence, the post independent India not only advanced in the field of technology (either by technology import or indigenous self sufficiency in technology); but also developed a rich army of skilled manpower by sponsoring training institutes and by augmenting the process of education.[3] Yet, what is achieved in terms of human resources development is marginal taking into account the vast population and the labour force that India can boast of. It is pertinent to observe that the unemployment problem is becoming increasingly insurmountable, because unlike the mid-decades of post- independence India, currently the number of unemployed is constantly in the rise.[4] There is a dearth of employment for those who received general education rather than technical and professional training. This can be attributed as a reason for the current concern shown by the Government of India towards vocationalizing its educational policy under the Human Resources Development Programme.

The launching of industrialization on a large scale after independence and the consolidation of the industrial work force after a century and four decades of industrialization process should have resulted in some improvements in the characteristics of the Indian labour force in terms of migration and commitment. The migration prior to independence was deemed to be rural-urban exodus. But with industrialization migration became a movement of job seekers from underdeveloped areas to developing areas. The unequal distribution of industrialization in the country and the concomitant economic disparity nevertheless contributed to such migration. The sons of the soil policy of recruitment which is gaining momentum as a public demand can be understood, as an opposition to such large scale migration.[5] So it can be contented that, the migrating character of Indian Labour force has remained unaltered.

Further, on the commitment front, the Indian labour force might have traversed a long way on the commitment continuum towards attachment to an industrial way of life. Yet, some very disturbing trends like absenteeism, whose rate is constantly on the rise, could be severely viewed in the light of commitment. The traditional village nexus might have decreased in its effect; yet, the commitment of the industrial workforce appear to be not high in view of the grave problem of absenteeism[6] in the industries.

Trade Unionism in Independent India

As has been observed in the previous chapter, trade unionism after initial trials and tribulations emerged as a collective force of working class movement during post industrialization and pre-independent India. The independent India had organised trade unions in its industrial sector and most of the major federations had come up by 1948.[7]

With the rise in the level of industrialization, the number of trade unions and their membership involvement also increased which is evident from the Table 3.5. The table indicates that, the number of unions in 1947-48 which was 2766 has increased to 36,925 in the year 1985 thereby registered a growth rate of 13.34 times. Contrarily, the membership involvement though registered as increase from 16.63 lakhs in 1947-48 to 76.85 lakhs in 1985, yet the increase is only by 4.62 times. So, the data indicates that the per union involvement has decreased since 1947-48.

The extent of unionization in organised sector which was 22.14 per

Table 3.5 : Number and Membership of Trade Unions

Year	*No. of Regd. Trade Unions*	*No. of Unions submitting returns*	*Total Membership in lakhs*
1947–48	2,766	1629 (58.89)	16.63
1951–52	4,623	2556 (55.29)	19.96
1955–56	8,095	4006 (49.70)	22.75
1960–61	11,312	6813 (60.22)	40.13
1966 April–Dec.	14,686	7244 (49.32)	43.92
1970 April–Dec.	20,879	8537 (40.88)	51.20
1974 April–Dec.	28,648	9800 (34.20)	61.90
1979 April–Dec.	34,430	10021 (29.10)	74.74
1980 April–Dec.	34,820	10294 (29.56)	74.95
1984 April–Dec.	36,630	11019 (30.08)	76.25
1985 April–Dec.	36,925	11325 (30.67)	76.85

Source : B.P. Tyagi, ***Economics and Social Welfare***, Meerut : Jayaprakash Nath & Co., 1986, p. 164.

cent (22.75 lakhs of union workers out of the total work force of 102.74 lakhs) in the year 1955-56 had registered a marginal growth to 30.67 per cent (76.85 lakhs out of 250.56 lakhs) in the year 1985-86. Thus the rest 70 per cent of work force engaged in organized sector are non-unionized.

Despite the growth in the number of trade unions and unionized employees, trade unions in India suffer from multifarious problems. Right from its infancy till the present, trade unions in India have been fully politicized. Every party whether in power or not foster trade unions on party ideologies. Under multiparty political structure, the trade union structure also is characterized by multiplicity.[8] The trade union leadership in India is dominated by outsiders.[9] Most of these leaders are either big name leaders or professional leaders. Professional leaders play a political apprenticeship in trade unions and big name leaders on account of their political status are invited to lead trade unions. Such political dominance, though unavoidable, results in inter and intra-union rivalries based both on political considerations and personality clashes. This weakens the organizational strength of unions as they get fragmented and fictionalized. Very often, it is believed that these leaders serve the cause of the political party and of their own position as a leader than serving the cause of the workers.[10]

The multiplicity and mushroom growth of unions and the decrease in the per union membership enrolment figures, weakens the financial position of unions. The organizational weakness of unions is evident from the fact that, less than the one third of unions submit their annual returns (Table 3.5). With regard to involvement of workers in trade union activities, there is a strong notion that, the workers attitude range from some amount of interest[11] to apathy and even to hostility.[12] But there is a consensus on the contention that the Indian workers totally lack union involvement.[13] The workers tend to believe that unions are to bargain on behalf of them and not with their help and involvement. This tendency is considered as the cause for low involvement of workers in union activities. All the above account portray Indian trade unionism as not a very strong collective force of the working class.

The Industrial Relations Functions

In the light of the profile of the Indian Trade Unionism, a comprehensive discussion on the industrial relations scenario of the country is essential to understand how the management of trade unions and industrial relations has assumed importance as a core functional area of personnel profession. In the first few years after independence, India witnessed a spate of work stoppages (Table 3.6) while still bearing the pains of partition. The enactment of Industrial Disputes Act, in the year 1947 virtually steered the industrial relations policy of the country towards Government intervention. The initial industrial relations scenario which was quite disturbed was responsible to stifle the lone voice of the then labour minister of the country and a great trade unionist late V.V. Giri who advocated for free collective bargaining as opposed to state intervention in resolving industrial disputes through conciliation and adjudication. Khandubhai Desai, who succeeded Giri (after he left the berth in the Ministry on protest) proclaimed finally that complete *laissez faire* is out of date. Society cannot allow workers or managements to follow the law of jungle. Therefore, as a last resort, the government has taken powers to refer disputes to adjudication. Thus once for all state intervention became the marked feature of industrial relations in India.

Table 3.6 : Industrial Disputes During 1947–1950

Year	*No. of Disputes*	*Mandays lost*
1947	1811	16562666
1948	1259	7837173
1949	920	6000595
1950	814	12806704

Source : Subramaniam, Labour Management, p. 212.

Collective bargaining on the other hand has remained purely voluntary.[14] This voluntary nature apparently gives freedom to the management and union to negotiate without external interference.

Whatever scope is left out for collective bargaining to play a role in industrial relations as both dispute preventing and settling mechanisms is getting vitiated by the absence of criteria for recognising trade unions[15] as bargaining agents and by the mutual conflict between the unions for getting recognition. The multiplicity of unions, politicization and dominance of outside leadership, inter and intra-union rivalries and such other weaknesses of trade unions still precipitate the crisis in industrial relations.

Militancy of unions jeopardizing healthy collective bargaining and breeding inter-union rivalries are on the increase. The strategy of strike is very often used, despite the curbs under the Industrial Disputes Act, 1947, more to serve the cause of union leadership than the interests of the workers. Lockouts are also on the increase.[16] And the entire industrial relations scenario is deteriorating gradually. (Table 3.7).

Table 3.7 : Industrial Disputes and Mandays lost during 1951–1989.

Year	*No. of Disputes*		*Mandays lost (in Millions)*	
1951	1071	(100)	3.82	(100)
1956	1203	(112.32)	6.99	(182.98)
1961	1357	(126.70)	4.92	(128.79)
1966	2556	(238.66)	13.85	(362.56)
1971	2752	(256.96)	16.55	(433.25)
1976*	1459	(136.28)	12.75	(323.77)
1981	2589	(241.74)	36.58	(957.59)
1986 (P)	1581	(147.62)	22.12	(579.06)
1988 (P)	N.A.		32.10	(840.31)
1989 (P) (Jan. to Sept.)	N.A.		14.59	(381.93)

* 1976 is the year of National Emergency.

N.A. : Not Available
P. : Provisional

Source : Labour Bureau, Simla and Economic Survey, 1989–90, Government of India.

The Table indicates that there is constant increase in both the frequency and severity rates of industrial disputes in the country cover the period 1951 to 1989. The index of frequency rate has increased by around 1.5 times during the period 1951-1986. The index of severity rate has increased by around 8.5 times during the same period.

A causewise analysis of the disputes will make important revelations having significant impact on the functions of personnel professional. The Table 3.8 provides the cause-wise distribution of disputes for the period 1947 to 1986. The causes are broadly bifurcated into economic and non-economic categories. Under economic category issues relating to wages

Table 3.8 : Cause-wise Distribution of Industrial Disputes in Percent Value (1947–1986)

Year	*Economic Causes (Wages & Bonus)*	*Non-Economic Causes*			*Total No. of disputes for which causes are known*
		Personnel	Indiscipline and violence	Misc.	
1947	42.9	24.7	--	32.4	1794
1948	39.7	37.9	--	22.4	1247
1949	38.0	34.8	--	27.2	865
1950	37.9	24.4	--	29.7	781
1951	36.2	37.5	--	26.3	1026
1952	40.5	42.6	--	16.9	933
1953	37.9	42.6	--	19.5	730
1954	36.7	46.9	--	16.4	801
1955	41.9	37.8	--	20.3	1124
1956	37.1	45.4	--	17.5	1103
1957	43.2	35.9	--	20.9	1556
1958	42.0	36.2	--	21.8	1514
1959	37.4	32.8	--	29.8	1492
1960	47.6	27.1	--	25.3	1506
1961	37.3	32.3	--	30.4	1314
1962	42.5	25.9	--	31.6	1474
1963	37.8	30.5	--	31.7	1466
1964	42.8	29.4	--	27.8	2122
1965	43.4	29.8	--	26.8	1825
1966	49.0	27.7	--	23.3	2536
1967	50.8	24.6	--	24.6	2760
1968	47.8	30.1	3.2	18.9	2717
1969	46.0	28.8	3.8	21.4	2609
1970	47.7	27.7	3.8	20.3	2843
1971	48.4	24.4	3.6	23.6	2723
1972	48.4	25.6	5.1	29.1	3153
1973	44.4	25.8	5.7	24.1	3296
1974	42.3	28.1	6.2	23.4	2863
1975	40.0	32.1	8.9	19.0	1911
1976	37.2	32.8	9.9	20.1	1418
1977	46.4	25.2	8.8	19.6	2964
1978	38.6	26.2	10.7	24.5	3094
1979	40.7	24.1	9.1	26.1	2906
1980	35.7	26.5	8.9	28.9	2698
1981	38.1	24.2	9.9	27.8	2453
1982	36.9	23.8	12.1	27.2	2412
1983	34.9	24.0	13.8	27.3	2407
1984	35.8	21.5	14.0	28.7	2005
1985 (P)	29.8	24.9	16.1	29.2	1700
1986 (P)	31.2	25.1	14.2	29.5	1531

P : Provisional -- : Denotes not available

Source : Labour Bureau, Simla.

and bonus are covered. The non-economic causes are trifurcated into personnel; indiscipline and violence; and miscellaneous categories. It is indicated by the table that, though the non-economic causes account for majority of the disputes, yet, wages and bonus as economic causes retain in status of the single most cause of industrial disputes in the country. It is highly relevant to note that the areas in personnel management account for around one third of the disputes. And since, 1968, indiscipline and violence emerged as a separate cause. The figures in this category which was 3.2 in 1968 gradually increased touching the highest i.e., 16.1 in 1985. Thus for personnel professionals to-day, issues arising out of managing people at work are becoming more and more prone to challenges and disputes. Indiscipline and violence are becoming increasingly difficult problems to deal within the sphere of industrial relations.

Labour Legislations in Post-Independent India

After Independence the Government enacted a number of labours laws to protect and improve the labour standards and to maintain industrial peace. The laws which primarily aimed at protecting labour standards and improving the working conditions enacted during this period are, Factories Act, 1948; Minimum wages Act, 1948; Dock Workers' Regulation of Employment Act, 1948; Plantation Labour Act, 1951 ; The Mines Act, 1952; Merchant Shipping Act, 1958; Motor Transport Workers; Act, 1961; Apprenticeship Act, 1961; Contract Labour (Regulation and Abolition) Act, 1970. The only and most important Act to regulate employee-employer relationship was the Industrial Disputes Act, 1947 which provided for the methods of settling industrial disputes. The various social security legislations enacted during this period are: Employees' State Insurance Act, 1948, Coal Mines Provident Fund, and Bonus Scheme Act, 1948; Employees Provident Fund Act, 1952 and the Central Maternity Benefit Act, 1961; Payment of Bonus Act, 1965; Payment of Gratuity Act, 1972. The compliance requirements under all these enactments and those of enacted prior to independence has become an important core area of personnel management function.

The significant contribution to the personnel profession however came from the Factories Act, 1948 which provided the institution of Welfare Officers under section 49. Similar provisions were also made under the Mines Act and Plantation Labour Act.[17]

Welfare Officer

The Factories, Act, 1948 which provided the institution of Welfare Officer, empowered the State Governments to make rules in prescribing the qualifications, duties and conditions of service of such officers. In order to facilitate the State Governments the Central Government framed the Welfare Officers' (Recruitment and Conditions of Service) Model Rules, 1951 and revised in 1957.[18] The qualifications prescribed by the Rules are, a degree of a university, a degree or diploma in social science and adequate knowledge of the language[19] spoken by the majority of workers employed in the factory. The conditions of service for the Welfare Officers interalia prescribed a status equivalent to the other departmental heads, a right to appeal to the state Government in case of discharge or dismissal by the occupier—a notion of protection of employment. Summarising the duties of a Welfare Officer provided under the Rules it can be observed that, the Welfare Officer has direct responsibility for the administration of service pertaining to welfare and benefits, health and safety, joint committees and leave with wages. He is also required to be concerned with the implementation of labour laws, proper working conditions, harmonious labour relations, industrial peace, plant productivity and workers' well-being. For this purpose he has to act as an adviser, counsellor, mediator and liaison man both to the management and labour.[20]

The Model Rules in prescribing the qualifications, duties and conditions of service while aimed at making the functioning of the Welfare Officers smooth and efficient; in actual practice it made the Welfare officer's function difficult and their position controversial. The Rules made in 1951 and various State Rules made in later years have not brought out any significant changes in spite of the shortcomings noticed in these years from the working experience of the Welfare Officers.

The first two qualifications prescribed for the Welfare Officer i.e., the University degree and diploma in social science are ambiguous.[21] With regard to the status given under the Rules, it may be well-intended but in practice as has been seen it becomes meaningless. Because the Welfare Officer's position is relegated to such other officers like Labour/Personnel and Industrial Relations. The provision of giving protection of employment is also not free from criticism. The protection accorded to the Welfare

Officer makes him an outsider to the management group, pushes him outside the managerial hierarchy, blocks his promotion possibilities and reduces his job to a blind alley position.[22]

A close perusal of the elaborate list of duties prescribed will bring to the fore such phrases like 'hold consultation'. ' bring to the notice of the factory management', 'study and understand', ' help and interpret', 'watch industrial relations', 'advise workers and management', 'maintain an impartial attitude', 'advise and assist in supervision', 'help workers to adjust to working environment', 'encourage formation of committees' etc. clearly indicate that the Welfare Officer has very little executive functions, if he has any at all. His role is to advice, counsel, suggest, watch, study, interpret and maintain a neutral role without taking sides.[23] This neutrality stance expected of the Welfare Officers resulted in acquiring some stigmata, such as, 'third force',[24] 'linking pin',[24] 'buffer zone', 'fire-fighter', 'non-aligned professional',[26] etc. The role of the Welfare Officer has been described as peripheral errand running chores[27] and as a post box for complaints by workers and as a convenience to other departments for issues show cause notices of indiscipline, pleading with department for allowing leave to workers . . . . in some extreme cases serving as intelligent officer about possible unrest among labour.[28] Such a low profile of the Welfare Officer is attributable to the management's obnoxious role in making the Welfare Officer a non-entity, line executives' intolerance to staff advice,[29] union's lack of faith, Government's apathy to review the provisions related to Welfare Officer's service conditions and above all the incumbent's negative contribution to the effectiveness of the officer.[30]

It is pertinent to observe that the duty chart of the Welfare Officer can be trifurcated into three core functions, namely, welfare, personnel administration and industrial relations. However, the functions of hiring and firing and disciplining on behalf of the management have been excluded apparently to maintain the neutrality position of the Welfare Officers. In reality many organisations have assigned these roles to the Welfare Officers which prompted the National Commission on Labour to observe that "the Welfare Officer should not be made to work as an agency to handle labour disputes on behalf of the management".[31]

Further, it was firmly believed that, the Welfare Officers were burdened with various duties covering the three areas of industrial relations, labour welfare and personnel management. It was urged by the erstwhile Labour Minister, Government of Bombay at the First All India Conference of Labour and Welfare Officers' 1953, that, "these three functions are well defined spheres and they need not be joined in one and the same person". He advocated the creation of personnel department in each sizeable undertaking.[32] However, by 1951 the Personnel Officer designation[33] was in the offing. It only gained currency during the late 1950s and early 1960s when more and more number of industries started with personnel as a separate department looking after labour welfare, industrial relations and personnel administration functions.

The emergence of personnel designation totally eclipsed the labour and welfare orientation in the Indian industries. The import of American and British know-how in human resources management can be a strong reason for the personnel designation dominating over the welfare and labour. By late 1960s the survey made by Committees on Labour Welfare appointed by National Commission on Labour strongly contended that one of the officers of the personnel department can be deputed to look after the functions usually performed by the Welfare Officer, because in its survey the Committee found that a number of establishments have dovetailed the functions of Welfare Officers with personnel department.[34] The Committee for this recommended that there is no necessity of appointing a Welfare Officer solely for the purpose of looking after welfare activities rather such an officer can be a part and parcel of the management. Thus from welfare the nomenclature came to be termed as personnel.

Development of the Personnel Discipline

Personnel management in India, as elsewhere, had its moorings in welfare and social work.[35] Social work as a problem solving technique came to be useful in almost all settings including industry.[36] The typical problems of personnel management and industrial relations, however, could not be adequately tackled by social work techniques alone. The problems were not only human in nature but also involved technology, structure, management, market, unions, consumer demands and many other environmental factors. As a result the personnel discipline embodied many managerial activities, not simply the welfare of the workers.

With the expansion of activities of personnel management, many new disciplines came into application. As a result, the traditional social work orientation got a serious set back. The emerging personnel discipline in the post independence India came under increasing influence of many social sciences like sociology, psychology, economics, law, ethics, politics, medicine, etc. With the greater exposure to the American and European management science, the personnel management became more a part of business management and the discipline emerged as a part of management education. The trend in 1970s that demonstrated the role and responsibilities of the personnel executives as members of the management team greatly subscribes to the management orientation of personnel discipline. As a result, 'personnel social work' gave place to the management orientation.[37]

Of late a new direction and enrichment in its quality as a discipline is emerging with the increasing impact of behavioural sciences in human resources management. It is pertinent to observe that after independence, the Indian academics as well as professions and increasing exposure to American Management education,[38] thereby incorporating the managerial sciences both in theory and practice.

In the initial stages of this adoptation process, personnel management in India delegently adhered to the western theories. But gradually a tendency developed among the academics and professionals to validate the western theories in the Indian context. The characteristics of India labour, their commitment, culture, motivational denominators vis-a-vis the management culture were well researched topics during 1950s and 1960s.[39] A band of industrial psychologists analysed the expectations, the need gap areas, job satisfaction, morale and motivation of the workers.[40] Social psychologists and sociologists resorted to empiricism as an important tool for understanding and analysing the personnel at work, their relations, behaviour and efficiency.[41] In situ research resorting to in-depth case analyses characterized most of the studies in Industrial relations. Trade Unionism, Collective Bargaining, Participative Management, Industrial strife, grievance and discipline are the specific areas which have received attention in industrial relations.[42]

The impact of research methodology, a wide and wild jungle of management theory, and above all behaviouralism opened new vistas of research, consultancy and management development programmes in India. Currently, over the lase decade there has been a mushroom growth of research and text book publications in personnel management and industrial relations. The text books mostly compiled theories advanced in the West and some of them provided indigenous cases in support of theory.[43] Analysis of practice, problem solving exercises, retrospective and prospective studies, experience based judgement findings on situations by practitioners and academicians embody the studies and analyses in personnel management to-day. There is also a spurt in the publication of Indian journals devoted to the problems of personnel management, industrial relations and labour welfare which by bringing out the findings of the professionals and academicians have augmented the growth of professional literature. A list of periodicals published in India is given in Annexure-II.[44] However, the personnel theory in India is unable to be culture specific due to obsession with imitation rather than innovation. So it can be concluded that the volume of the personnel discipline has increased in leaps and bounded, while its quality in India needs lots of improvement.

Personnel management is not only a theory but also a skill required for practice of human resource management. So like any other management profession, personnel profession too demands training facilities for imparting both the knowledge and skill.

Training Facilities in Personnel Management

There were only two institutes prior to independence at Bombay and Calcutta which imparted some training to labour officers with social work and welfare orientation. Soon after independence some more institutes with social work and welfare orientation emerged. Thereafter many institutes and university departments have come up which can be trifurcated into social work institutes, pure personnel management and industrial relations institutes and the management institutes. The Tables 3.9, 3.10, 3.11 provide details about these institutes besides enlisting few institutes offering short term refresher courses (Table 3.12).

It can be seen from the above tables that the School/Departments of Social Work marked a relatively earlier beginning than the Labour Schools or Management Institutes. The emergence of Social Work Institutes soon

Table 3.9 : Institutes having Social Work Nomenclature

S. No.	*Name of the Institute*	*Degree Awarded*	*Year of Establish-ment*
1.	Institute of Social Sciences, Kasividyapitha	P.G. Degree in Social Work	1947
2.	Delhi School of Social Work	P.G. Degree in Social Work	1947
3.	Deptt. of Sociology & Social Work, Lucknow University.	P.G. Degree in Social Work	1949
4.	Faculty of Social Work, M.S. Universty, Baroda	P.G. Degree in Social Work and P.G. Diploma in IRPM	1950
5.	Madras School of Social Work	P.G. Degree in Social Work	1952
6.	Xavier Institute of Social Sciences, Ranchi	P.G. Degree in Social Work	1955
7.	Institute of Social Science, Agra	P.G. Degree in Social Work	1956
8.	Dept. of Social Work and Sociology, Andhra University	P.G. Degree in Social Work	1957
9.	P.S.G. School of Social Work, Coimbatore	P.G. Degree in Social Work	1958
10.	Udaipur School of Social Work, Udaipur	P.G. Degree in Social Work	1959
11.	Indore School of Social Work	P.G. Degree in Social Work	1960
12.	School of Social Work, Mangalore	P.G. Degree in Social Work	1961
13.	Institute of Social Work, Alwyae.	P.G. Degree in Social Work	1961
14.	Department of Social Work, Stella Maris Collge, Madras	P.G. Degree in Social Work	1962
15.	Dept. of Social Work, Karnataka University Dharwar.	P.G. Degree in Social Work	1962
16.	Dept. of Social Work, Loyala College, Madras	P.G. Degree in Social Work	1963

Contd..

Table 3.9 : Contd...

S. No.	Name of the Institute	Degree Awarded	Year of Establishment
17.	College of Social Work, Jamia Milia Islamia,Delhi	P.G. Degree in Social Work	1970
18.	Dept. of Social Work Jamia Milia Islamia, Delhi	P.G. Degree in Social Work	N.A.
19.	University of Poona	P.G. Degree in Social Work	N.A.
20.	Shivaji University, Kollhapur	P.G. Degree in Social Work	N.A.
21.	University of Kerala	P.G. Degree in Social Work	N.A.
22.	Visva Bharati, Shanti Niketan	P.G. Degree in Social Work	N.A.
23.	Kamaraj University, Madurai	P.G. Degree in Social Work	N.A.
24.	Mysore University, Mysore	P.G. Degree in Social Work	N.A.

N.A. : Not available.
Source : Compiled from Secondary Sources.

after independence till the early 1960s is probably due to the fact that the personnel discipline heavily relied upon the social work orientation. Simultaneously, however, separate labour welfare departments started as in case of Patna University in collaboration with the Cornell University, U.S.A. This was necessitated by the provision of Welfare Officer under the Factories, Mines and Plantations Acts. In some Universities Labour Welfare Departments emerged as a splinter group of social work and sociology, like that of Andhra University and Utkal University. The Labour Welfare Departments preferred to concentrate on the human problems in industrial organisations unlike the social work schools who made industry one of the many settings in which problems could be solved by the application of social work techniques. With the emergence and growth of management education in India notably after 1962, even the labour welfare departments tilted towards management orientation and switched over to such nomenclatures as Industrial Relations and Personnel Management. Thus, the institutional facilities available for imparting training in personnel discipline have become quite wide and varied.

Table 3.10 : Institutes Having Personnel Management/Industrial Relations/Labour Welfare Nomenclature

S. No.	*Name of the Institute*	*Degree Awarded*	*Year of Establish-ment*
1.	Bombay Labour Institute	P.G. Degree in Labour Welfare	1947
2.	Dept. of Labour and Social Welfare, Patna University	P.G. Degree in Labour & Social Welfare	1948
3.	Xavier Labour Relations Institute, Jamshedpur	2 years P.G. Diploma in Industrial Relations	1950
4.	Dept. of Labour Welfare, Gujarat University, Ahmedabad	P.G. Degree in Labour Welfare	1958
5.	Dept. of Labour & Social Welfare (LSW), Bhagalpur	P.G. Degree in L.S.W.	1959
6.	Dept. of Industrial Relation & Personnel Management (IRPM), Berhampur Uni.	P.G. Degree in I.R.P.M.	1967
7.	Dept. of Labour Welfare, Utkal University.	P.G. Degree in Labour Welfare	1971
8.	Dept. of IRPM, Andhra University, Visakhapatnam	P.G. Degree in I.R.P.M.	1975
9.	Guru Ghasi Das University, Bilaspur	P.G. Degree in Industrial Relations	N.A.
10.	Dept. of PM & IR, Tata Institute of Social Sciences	P.G. Degree in I.R.P.M.	N.A.
11.	Punjab University	P.G. Degree in PM & IR 1 year P.G. Diploma in PM & IR	N.A.
12.	University of Delhi	1 year P.G. Diploma in Personnel Management.	N.A.
13.	Guru Nanak Dev University	Diploma in Labour Laws and Labour Administration.	N.A.
14.	Himachal Pradesh University	1 year P.G. Diploma in PM & LW	N.A.

(Contd.)

Table 3.10 : (Contd.)

S. No.	*Name of the Institute*	*Degree Awarded*	*Year of Establishment*
15.	University of Jodhpur	Diploma in Labour Laws, Personnel Management and Labour Welfare.	N.A.
16.	Kakatiya University	Diploma in PM & IR	N.A.
17.	Kurukshetra University	P.G. Diploma in PM & LW	N.A.
18.	Mohanlal Sukhadia University, Baroda	Diploma in Labour Law and Personnel Management	N.A.
19.	Nagpur University	Diploma in IR & PM	N.A.
20.	University of Rajasthan	Dip. in Labour Law, Labour Welfare and Personnel Mgt.	N.A.
21.	Aligarh University	Dip. in Labour Laws, and Labour Relations	N.A.
22.	NIPM, Calcutta	P.G. Diploma in PM and IR	N.A.
23.	Annamalai University	1 year Dip. in Personnel Mgt. (by correspondence course)	N.A.

N.A. : Not Available

Source : Compiled from secondary sources.

Table 3.11 : Management Institutes in India

S.No.	*Name of the Institute*	*Degree Awarded*
1.	Indian Institute of Management, Calcutta	MBA with Specialization in IRPM.
2.	IIM, Ahmedabad	MBA, Specialization in PM & OB.
3.	IIM, Bangalore	MBA, Specialization in IRPM
4.	IIM, Lucknow	MBA, Specialization in PM & IR
5.	Birla Institute of Technology, Ranchi.	MBA, Specialization in PM & OB
6.	Jamnalal Bajaj Institute of Management Studies, Bombay	MBA

Source : Compiled from secondary sources.

Table 3.12 : Institutes Offering Short-term and Refresher Courses

1.	Bombay Labour Institute.
2.	National Labour Institute, Delhi.
3.	Sri Ram Centre for Industrial Relations and Human Resources, New Delhi.
4.	National Productivity Council, New Delhi.
5.	Ahmedabad Textile Industry's Research Association, Ahmedabad.
6.	South India Textile Industry's Research Association, Coimbatore.
7.	All India Management Association, New Delhi.

Sources : Compiled from Secondary sources

Contemporary Professional Stature of Perso-nnel Management

It can be observed from the tracings of history made in this and previous chapters that, personnel management had emerged after an evolutionary change over after industrialisation and still it is under a flux. Some call it an occupation in conflict and others call it an emerging profession. In this context, the professional status of the personnel management currently need to be projected. In order to do this, three basic questions are addressed here:

i) What is the nomenclature by which the profession is known and how it has emanated ?

ii) What is the professional status of personnel executive inside and outside the organisation ?

iii) What are the arrangements made to organise and sustain the professional body of personnel executives ?

Varied Nomenclature and Identity Crisis

The evolution marked in the growth of personnel management has resulted in many nomenclatures and designations of personnel profession over a period of time. To-day, the personnel department is known by such other nomenclatures as labour office, labour personnel office, Industrial Relations Department, Welfare Department, etc. The size and structure of the organisation and the management culture associated with sectorial differences can be attributed as causes for different nomenclatures. Small organisations in co-operative sector often adopt labour or welfare designation. Large public sector find it imperative to have split function departments each looking after one or more core areas of personnel management. Depending on the nomenclatures, the designations of personnel executives also very. An illustrative list of such designations are personnel manager/officer, labour officer, labour personnel officer, Welfare officer, industrial relations officer, labour welfare officer, etc.[45] The prefixes of Chief, Deputy, Assistant, Senior, Junior etc. are made to these designations denoting the hierarchical position of those executives.

Despite this lack of uniformity a clear cut functional divisional of the personnel activities has emerged namely, "the three areas of labour welfare, industrial relations and personnel administration are being looked after by three professional functionaries; labour officer, welfare officer and personnel officer"[46] This is of course not uniform in all industrial establishments. There are integrated, split function and extended departments.[48] All the three functions are combined and assigned to single department, thereby making such departments integrated[47] ones. There are also experiences where separate departments are created to take independent charge of the three core functions of personnel management. Instances of assigning many extraneous functions to the personnel department over and above the three core functions were also rampant in small organisations either in private or co-operative sectors. Such departments are extended ones.

Besides these categories many traditional personnel functions are either receiving the status of separate functions as in case of training and development, or are being looked after by outside consultants like that of legal and recruitment functions. And contrarily some new functions are getting added to personnel management with the increasing influence of behaviouralism and artificial intelligence mechanism like computers. Thus not only in their nomenclature but also in their functional activities the departments present a kaleidoscopic picture.

The variedness in the designation of officers, in the nomenclature of departments and in the functional distributions within the departments, can be taken as a reflection of the company demands on personnel profession. And to meet these demands, probably, the institutional training facilities do also have a varied structure and nomenclature. Thus, though currently personnel is the most widely used nomenclature to denote the profession dealing with people at work; yet, its identity is very often nebulous due to the erosion by many other nomenclatures and designations. The most powerful nomenclature which is currently gaining momentum is "Human Resources Management" (HRM) or even Human Resources Development (HRD). In India what started as a macro level policy decision[49], HRD, at the micro level gained popularity as a management development and training function. Currently there is a strong favourability towards the HRD nomenclature. However, whether HRD will be able to eclipse the personnel nomenclature or not, time alone will prove. Yet predictions can be done. And that is attempted in a later chapter.

Status of the Personnel Officer inside and outside the Organisation

The genesis of personnel function as discussed so far, indicates that the designation of Welfare Officer and his status as defined under the statutes had, won such stigmata as 'third force', 'buffer zone, 'non-aligned professional' etc. However, the personnel designation and the status of personnel officer in the organisations has made it a part and parcel of the organisation's functional structure. Today any organisation structure embodies personnel as a distinct functional division or department. Thus personnel management has come to be treated as a management function and personnel officer as a part of the management team. The coexistence of both welfare and personnel officers has not changed this position, because welfare is insubordinated to personnel by defining personnel as a promotional channel for the welfare officer. Nevertheless, the incumbents to the office of welfare officer after years of uncertainty of their official status (for which the status are responsible) have preferred to be identified with the management team. Thus by whatever nomenclature the personnel department is designated, it has remained as a part of management structure.

The ascribed status of welfare officer as defined by status has not been really achieved. Because contrary to the specifications that, the welfare officer should be given appropriate status corresponding to the status of other executive heads of the factory, he is relegated to a supervisory category or junior managerial position. This has not improved much in case of personnel designation to. Personnel departments as are organised in the industrial either receive an independent status or insubordinated to the line or staff coordinates ones. In case of line insubordinated or staff coordinated departments, the status of personnel head is relegated to middle management level. Even in cases where the personnel department is an independent one, it is not given the status ascribed to other heads of the department in line division and even in other staff departments.

The ubiquitous[50] nature of personnel function makes it all pervasive.[51] And all those who deal with the human resources, take decisions effecting the human beings are personnel executives in their own right.[52] The personnel work of an organisation cannot be housed within a certain department bearing the exalted name. Rather it is a leaven permeating all phases of management, the responsibility for which rests upon all executives and persons in supervisory positions.[53] Thus in personnel management there are some who really decide and act, while others only render advice, assist and help in personnel decision-making and execution. The personnel department in this bifurcation of role boundaries performs the later one for this reason is known as a staff department[54] in relation to the line department[55] which in fact play the former role. The interaction between the line departments and the personnel staff generates lots of heat, some times resulting into open conflict. The reasons for the line-staff conflict in personnel function are adequately summarised by Earnest Dale as under:

- "Failure of line to understand staff role.
- Lack of line cooperation and failure to use staff.
- Staff assumes or duplicates line authority.
- Staff operates in extremes — either it dictates or it is too weak.
- Staff policy often confuses the line".[56]

It is the practice that line managers mostly make to the top. Such top executives tend to show preferential treatment to the line executives over the staff. The placement of the personnel department in organisation structures bears testimony to this contention. Thus the Chief Executive Officer can be blamed for generating conflict between the line executives and personnel executives instead of balancing their relationships.[57]

Whatever be the reason of line-staff conflict, its effect on the status of personnel department in the organisations is crucial. In India, the staff role of the personnel department has been described as peripheral, errand-running chores,[58] and as a post box for complaints by workers and as a convenience to other departments for issuing show-cause notices for cases of indiscipline, pleading with departments for allowing leave to workers..... in some extreme cases serving as intelligence officers about possible unrest among labour.[59] The very fact that the personnel executives often come in direct contact with union leaders, earn for them the stigma of ' trouble shooters'. The official and procedural strings that the personnel executives pull in some personnel functions like recruitment, promotion, sanctioning of leave and benefits, etc. which are included under the establishment of employees, ostensibly makes them dubious 'power holders' and subject them to the criticism and envy of other staff and line departments.

In order to make the personnel departments more effective in their functioning many practitioners and researchers have made suggestions. While Billimoria,[60] Pande,[61] and Agarwal[62] suggest that the personnel head shall report to the top executive in order to be unfettered in tendering advice how-so-ever unpalatable it might be to the line executives; Chatterjee[63] argues in favour of the personnel managers' expertise, his persuasiveness and his willingness to help the line, rather than on his access to the top management. Rudrabasavaraj[64] and Agarwal[65] suggest an integrated approach requiring top executives' and line executives' favourable attitude towards the personnel department and the competence and ability of the personnel department of inspire such positive attitude. IIPM,[66] Roy[67] and Jacob[68] attribute the sole responsibility of making personnel advice acceptable and the personnel function respectable to the professional acumen of the personnel executive. Dayal[69] suggests mutual understanding and acceptance of each others' role boundary and perception by every role-incumbent of his multirole relationship. While Chatterjee[70] evaluates the possibility of role rotation as a method for bringing about line-staff compatibility, Jacob[71] and Tripathy[72] suggest for orientation, training and educating line in personnel functions.

All these, however, confirm the inevitability of line-staff dynamics in personnel function. What emerges is that, the status of personnel profession and its effectiveness is largely dependent upon the personality aura and other personnel characteristics of the personnel man. This raises serious doubt about the personnel profession depending solely on scientific knowledge and strong training base. Rather it has come to be treated as an art, though partially.

Reflecting on the status of personnel executives outside the organisation, it can be pointed out that as professional their services directly are useful more for specific organisations rather than the larger society.[73] Of course, indirectly serving an organisation can be a service to the society because modern society is organisational society. Yet, the utility of the skill and knowledge of the personnel professional for serving the common good of a larger section of the society is very limited. And, hence, the society does not keep the personnel profession in the same esteem as it assigns to the medical, law and such other professions. Thus the personnel executives enjoy only a quasi-professional status outside the organisation.

Organising and Sustaining the Professional Body of Personnel Executives

One important point to be considered with regard to the professional status of personnel management in India is that, as a body of professionals, the personnel executives organised themselves around eight years earlier to the management professional body. While the Indian Institute of Personnel Management (IIPM) was organised, in 1948, the All India Management Association (AIMA) was formed in 1956. The delay in the emergence of the professional body of management has been attributed to the reason that, the top managements of private companies mostly preferred to join the employers' organisations like Indian Federation of Chambers of Commerce and Industry, the All India Organisation of Industrial Employers. The All India Manufactures' Organisation and the Employers' Federation of India[74]. Rather with the emergence of public sector undertakings after India went into planned development in 1951, a new generation of managers grew and showed interest to form the All India Management Association.

In this context, the fact that the IIPM was started in July, 1948 soon after independence, goes to prove that the personnel profession took first step towards organising a body of professionals[75]. This body with its headquarters at Calcutta started with 17 branches at various industrial centres all over India. It was registered under the Societies Registration

Act, 1860 as a voluntary association of men and women engaged in personnel functions of management with the aim of persistently focusing the importance of human aspect of management. By the time of its merger with National Institute of Labour Management (NILM) in March 1980 it had 2500 corporate, Associate and Student members, about 70 institutional members distributed over 18 branches and a number of local groups. Its main objectives were enunciated as under:

- to develop and spread ideas concerning the human values and to serve as a forum for exchange of ideas and experiences and collection and dissemination of the principles, practices, techniques and methods regarding personnel management, industrial relations, and labour/social welfare and industrial jurisprudence in all their bearings.
- to promote the study of personnel and industrial relations problems, and
- to promote and safeguard the status and interest of personnel management, industrial relations and labour welfare work and of those engaged in the profession.

In order to achieve its aims and objectives, the IIPM was providing comments and suggestions to the central and state Governments and various commissions and committees on policy areas in personnel management. It was indulged in broadly four principal activities, namely:

a) Organising conferences and seminars,

b) Organising training programmes,

c) Undertaking research projects; and lastly,

d) turning out professional literature through its publication, titled 'Personnel Management in India' and 'Readings in personnel management' which have been acclaimed as the most useful publications on the subject in India. By publishing a bimonthly journal namely, "Industrial Relations", the IIPM used to bring about a fusion between theory and practice. Besides these major activities the IIPM in 1971 brought about a modern curriculum for training in personnel management after deliberation in the National Conference which was a tended by practising professionals and academicians.

The IIPM framed a code of ethics to which all its members wer required to pledge in order to be recognised as professionals. The cod of ethics of IIPM reads as under:

"Recognising and accepting the responsibilities of the profession of personnel management, I as a member of the Indian Institute of Personnel Management, shall —

— Uphold the honour and dignity of the profession and the Institute;

— Observe and maintain integrity as the key note of professional conduct and shall perform my professional duties with fairness, impartiality, fidelity and dedication to the cause of the profession ;

— Recognize and accept the dignity and worthy of an individual as a human being irrespective of race, religion, language, caste or creed, and strive for the development of his personality;

— Co-operate in maximizing the effectiveness of the profession by exchanging freely information and experience with others and by contributing to the development of the profession to the best of my ability;

— Maintain at all times an open mind with regard to problems that I have to deal with in the course of my work and approach the problems of others with understanding;

— Not allow any interest other than professional to interfere with my official work;

— Strive unceasingly for self-development by acquiring ever increasing knowledge, skill and experience related to the profession;

— Endeavour to extend public knowledge on professional

matters and try to eliminate misconceptions and misunderstandings about the profession;

— Express publicly an opinion on professional matters only when it is founded on adequate knowledge and honest conviction;

— Not damage, directly or indirectly, the professional reputation or practice of other members ;

— Exercise due restraint in criticizing the work of other members ;

— Endeavour to give credit for professional work to those to whom it is due;

— Endeavour to provide opportunities for the development and advancement of professional men who work with me;

— Uphold the principle of appropriate remuneration for those engaged in professional work;

— Not associate in work with another members who does not conform to ethical standards and not hesitate to bring to the notice of the Institute unethical practice adopted by any member of the Institute;

— Be faithful to my employer or client, and present clearly to him the consequences to be expected, if my professional advice is not accepted;

— Advice engagement of specialists when I am convinced that such services are in the best interests of my employer or client and shall cooperate with them in their work;

— Follow professional principles and practices tactfully and courageously keeping in mind the principles of equity in the fair distribution of work and rewards;

— Promote the concepts, methods, skills and techniques in the field that contribute to productivity, growth, profitability and employee satisfaction.

— Not disclose any information of a coincidental nature that I may acquire in the course of professional work without obtaining the consent of those concerned; and

— Not accept or offer any improper gratification in any form or manner whatsoever in connection with or in the course of my professional work".

Commanding the role of IIPM the National Commission on Labour observed that, "personnel management as a profession has acquired importance in the last 20 years and the credit for this goes to the Indian Institute of Personnel Management". A more or less contemporary institute which had played an important role towards professionalisation of personnel management was the National Institute of Labour Management (NILM). NILM was started around one and half year later to IIPM i.e. on 26th January 1950, with its headquarters at Bombay. The NILM in its objectives have the following :

- to foster and encourage and promote the development of cordial relations between employers and employees.
- to conduct investigations into different labour problems and to compile reports thereon.
- to undertake special study on existing labour legislation with a view to suggesting improvements and indicating lines, of future labour legislation.
- to pool the experience of members and to formulate the most effective methods for the administration of personnel policy.
- to arrange meetings for exchange of views and dissemination of knowledge and techniques of handing labour problems.
- to organise training and instruction in personnel management and to grant diplomas and proficiency certificates with a view to ensuring a high standard for the profession.
- to maintain and up-to-date library on labour and welfare subjects, and to supply information, bibliographies and references on subjects

relating to labour and welfare.

- to establish or aid in the establishment of funds to further the cause of the personnel management.

Compared with the objectives of IIPM, the NILM's objectives are more specific and practical. It sounds more as an action plan, whereas the IIPM's objectives are more broad based and appear like policy statements. The NILM in order to give expression to its objectives and had held several seminars and conferences on such topics as "the role of trade unions in planned economy", "the role of personnel officers in promoting better communication in industry", "executive training and development", "techniques of selection and interview of employees in industrial undertakings", "the role of personnel officer in prospect", "Personnel function in management development" and "opportunity and challenge of personnel management", etc. These topics speak about the concern that NILM had shown towards practical problems of managing people at work. Thus IIPM and NILM as independent professional bodies had made efforts to improve the status of personnel profession since the very beginning of India's Independence.

As epoch making event in the professionalisation of personnel management in India was the amalgamation of the erstwhile IIPM and NILM in March, 1980 into a singular body called National Institute of Personnel Management (NIPM), thereby strengthening the professional body further. Calcutta continued to be the head office of NIPM and corresponding status of membership was assigned to members of NILM and IIPM in the new body both at the head quarters level and at the various branch levels. The adhoc Central Executive Council of NIPM consisted of the representatives from both the NILM and IIPM at the beginning. Liabilities and assets of both the old professional bodies were integrated and placed under a Trust. However, it took a series of high level committees, starting with the Implementation Committee of IIPM and NILM (set up in terms of the resolutions adopted by their respective general bodies on 17th March 1979 i.e., prior to the amalgamations) till the appointment of a task force on 22nd June, 1987 for drafting the Constitution of NIPM. Incorporating the amendments of 19th March, 1983, 18th February, 1984, and 14th April, 1988 the final draft of the constitution was adopted by the general body of the NIPM on 18th February, 1989, which came out as a public document on 1st May, 1989. All these years till 1989 May, NIPM was consolidating itself procedurally and organisationally.

As enumerated in the constitution, NIPM addresses itself to 29 objectives given as under:

- to organise into an association of all persons engaged in or interested in or in connection with personnel management, industrial relations and labour welfare;
- to serve as a forum for exchange of ideas and experiences and collection and dissemination of information on management in general and personnel management, industrial relations and labour and social welfare, in particular;
- to spread the knowledge of the principles, practices, techniques and methods regarding personnel management, industrial relations and labour and social welfare and industrial jurisprudence in all their bearings;
- to sponsor, promote, encourage, conduct and contribute to the study and research and to impart instructions to any subject touching any or all aspects of personnel management, industrial relations, labour and social welfare, industrial legislations and industrial jurisprudence, including their social, psychological, political and economic background and context;
- to promote and safeguard the status and the interests of personnel management, industrial relations and labour welfare work and the interests of those engaged therein;
- to pool the experience of the members to encourage and promote the development of cordial relations between employers and employees;
- to establish and maintain libraries and equip them with books on subjects concerning management in general, and in particular on personnel management, industrial relations, industrial law and jurisprudence, labour and social welfare, all other allied and related subjects, and other publication, bulletins, records and journals;
- to promote, sponsor, submit, present deputations, memorials, petitions, representations to Local, State, Union and other authorities for

better laws and administration in all matters concerning any of the objects of the Institute and for healthy development of personnel management, industrial relations and labour welfare;

- to organise conference, seminars, meetings, discussions, debates, study courses, collection of statistics, exhibitions, shows, tours, trips and to establish trusts, endowments and scholarships for the promotion and furtherance of the aims and objects of the institute;
- to undertake special study of existing labour legislations with a view to suggesting improvements and indicating lines of future labour legislation;
- to represent the Institute and its interest before Local, State and Central authorities and other organizations, commissions, boards, enquiry bodies, etc. , in India and abroad;
- to publish, sell, distribute free or otherwise, journals, magazines, publications, bulletins, books, pamphlets, souveniers and the like in furtherance of the objects of the Institute and in any event not for the purpose of carrying trade therewith;
- to subscribe to, or affiliate, collaborate, co-operate and federate with any other society having these or similar objects either in part or in whole;
- to conduct training courses and/or examinations in one or more aspects of personnel management, allied subjects and to award appropriate Certificates and/or Diploma;
- to obtain any Charter, Provisional Order or Act of Parliament for enabling the Institute to carry on any of its objects into effect;
- to acquire by purchase, taking on lease or otherwise, lands and buildings, add all other properties, movable and immovable, which the Institute, for the purpose hereof, may think proper to acquire;
- to sell, improve, manage, develop, exchange, lease or let under lease, sub-let, mortgage, dispose of, turn to account or otherwise deal with, all or any part of the property of the institute;
- to construct upon any premises required for the purpose of the

institute any building or buildings for the purposes of the Institute and to alter, add to or remove any building or structure upon such premises;

- to raise any monies for the purpose of the Institute by way of special subscriptions, membership or entrance fees, donations, special fees, loans, debentures or in any other manner on such terms and conditions as may be determined;
- to create Trust and/or Foundations out of the Institute's own funds or donations, grants, gifts, or bequests made by any persons or institution specifically in that behalf for any particular purpose not inconsistent with the objects of the Institute and to establish or aid in the establishment of Funds for furthering the objects of the Institute;
- to accept from the Government, organisations, institutions and individuals grants, donations, subscriptions, gifts, bequests, endowments, special fees, etc. for the furtherance of the objects of the institute;
- to deposit any money or securities in the name of the Institute with any Bank/Post Office and withdraw the same;
- to invest money belonging to the Institute in security as permissible under the appropriate law;
- to execute, effect and do all such assurances, deeds and things as may be required to perfect or complete any instruments or documents whatsoever and to register the same;
- to demand, realise, recover, use for, receive and give effect to receipt and discharge for all monies, securities, debts, legacies, property and goods of or to which the Institute may become possessed or entitled to or which may become due or payable or transferable to the Institute from any person or persons, entities, organizations and authorities;
- to engage employees for the smooth and effective functioning of the Institute and to pay their remuneration and regulate terms and conditions of employment or engagement;

- to make from time to time bye-laws for the control, conduct and regulation of the affairs of the Institute;
- to generally do all such things as are incidental to and/or conducive to the attainment of the above objects or any of them.
- to take over the membership and activities of the Indian Institute of Personnel Management and the National Institute of Labour Management from the date of formation of the National Institute of Personnel Management, in terms of the resolutions adopted by the General Bodies of the above named Institutes on 17th March, 1979 at Hyderabad.

The list when carefully pursued and compared with the objectives of IIPM and NILM reveals that, NIPM has combined most of the objectives of the previous bodies and has included many objectives which are meant for guiding the operations of the professional body. Rather, a bulk of objectives in one way or the other are regulatory in nature. So it can be inferred that NIPM retains the spirit of the objectives of both IIPM and NILM.

In order to realise these objectives, the NIPM conducts National seminars at the branch levels, sponsors study teams collects and disseminates employment informations, holds essay competitions. The institute publishes monographs and research studies prepared by the members besides bringing out a quarterly journal titled 'Personnel Today'. Further, every branch brings out a monthly or bimonthly or quarterly news letters/ bulletins highlighting their performance. The NIPM has instituted one award namely. 'Most Distinguished Service Medal' for felicitating one person for his or her outstanding contribution to the institute and the profession.

Select members who distinguish themselves by rendering meritorious and outstanding service to the profession and to the cause of the institute are admitted as Fellows. So far, i.e., by 1988, 66 fellowships have been conferred on corporate/life members. Awards by Coal India, Orissa Branch Silver Jubilee Medal, EFI, AIOE, NIPM proficiency U.P. Branch, Karnataka Branch Silver Jubilee Medals and Tarneja Awards were instituted to motivate better performance in the diploma in personnel management courses offered by NIPM on all India basis. NIPM Medals are also awarded to the successful candidates who top in their respective institutions awarding degrees and diplomas in personnel management and Industrial Relations.

As on 30.9.1988, there were 39 branches including the Head quarters with a membership enrolment of 7125 life, corporate, associate, student and institutional members. And to this figure, another 855 members were added by 31.3.1989 under different categories of membership.[75]

The NIPM has outlined a new set of code of ethics to which every member pledges. The code of ethics is as follows:

"As a member of the National Institute of Personnel Management, I declare that I shall—

— subscribe to the aims and objectives of the National Institute of Personnel Management and be bound by its constitution;

— Recognise and accept the dignity of an individual as human being, irrespective of religion, language, caste or creed;

— Maintain high standards of integrity and behaviour demanded by the profession;

— Conduct myself as a responsible member of the management team committed to the achievement of the organizational goal;

— Take keen interest in the establishment of healthy personnel practices and development of the profession;

— Try to win confidence and gain respect of the employers and employees and make myself available to them to provide formal and informal intervention to resolve industrial conflicts;

— Endeavour to enhance the good name of my profession in dealing with other professional bodies, government departments, and employers; and employees' organisations.

— Co-operate in maximising the effectiveness of the profession by exchangii.g freely information and experience with other members;

— Not allow any interest other than professional to interfere with my official work;

— Not interfere with the right of association of the employees;

— Not disclose any information of a confidential nature that I may acquire in the course of may professional work without obtaining the consent of those concerned and shall not use confidential information for personal gains;

— Not accept or offer any improper gratification in any form or manner whatsoever in connection with or in the course of my professional work; and

— Not take or acquiesce in any such action which may bring the Institute and/or the profession into disrepute."

The NIPM has condensed the code of ethics as it has pruned down the twenty-one ethical pledgings of IIPM to thirteen. The IIPM's code of ethics sounds more like a set of do's and don'ts , whereas that of NIPM appears like commitments or pledgings. However, the content and spirit is more or less retained in the new code of ethics, though the format has been changed.

Summing up

The analysis of the current status of the personnel profession basing upon the facts since 1947 in India indicate that the personnel has been incorporated as a management function. The post independent period in India has witnessed a spurt in industrialisation, increase in the industrial workforce and trade unions. During this period the Government also added a number of personnel profession. The employers increasingly employed special trained personnel in the field not only to deal with the industrial workers and their unions but also to comply the provisions of the various Labour Laws.

During this period some of the labour laws (Factories Act, 1948, Plantation Act, 1951, Mines Act, 1952) made the provision for the appointment of welfare officers. The Government, through the Rules made under these Acts, prescribed the qualifications, duties and functions, status and remuneration of the welfare officers. Basing upon the analysis of the duties and functioning and status of the welfare officer it can be held that the Government probably wanted to create an ideal institution in the industrial organisations and had a lot of expectation from it. But in reality, the experience of the welfare officers indicate that Rules framed by the Government became contributory for their functioning difficult and position controversial. However, within few years from the creation of welfare officers, personnel designation appeared in the Indian scene. Any by late 1950, and early 1960s the use of the designation has become quite popular. The profession marked a major change with the creation of independent personnel department integrating the personnel, industrial relations and welfare functions. Gradually the labour and welfare orientation which dominated the profession in the pre-independent period got eclipsed.

The improvement in the discipline base of the profession is also noteworthy. Initially, as elsewhere personnel management as a discipline owed its origin to 'Social Work'. Later it came under the influence of various social sciences like psychology, sociology, economics, law etc. the post 1970s which saw advent of management literature and behavioural sciences in the west had also its impact in India which resulted in recognising personnel management as part of management education. Initially though personnel management largely adhered to the western literature, but gradually various scholars took up the task of validating the western theories in their application in Indian conditions. Inspite of the expansion in the research in the personnel and related areas, personnel discipline in India till date heavily depends upon the western literature.

Alongwith the transformation of the discipline from social work base to management, the educational institutes offering training to the personnel executives also brought out changes in their training programmes from social work/labour welfare to management orientation. There was also a change in the nomenclature with Industrial Relations and Personnel Management becoming popular among others.

Inspite of the emergence of personnel designation in the 1950s, currently it has remained confined mostly to the public sector and large scale Private Industrial undertakings. In the small and medium scale industries and the cooperative sector the department which shoulder the responsibility of performing the personnel function are identified by such nomenclatures like Labour Departments, Industrial Relations, Labour Welfare etc. Despite the lack of uniformity in the nomenclature, the three distinct functions of personnel management namely Personnel Administration, Industrial Relations and Labour Welfare have been clearly identified. Depending upon the size and form of organisation these functions are either carried out by independent departments or by one integrated department. Of late one designation which is gaining momentum is the 'Human Resources'.

The position of the welfare officer as a personnel functionary within the organisation still continues to be controversial. The Personnel Officer/ Manager, however, is not only being accepted as a part of the management team but invariably enjoys a higher occupational status than that of the Welfare Officer. Despite the acceptance of Personnel as a managerial function, its role is confined to rendering advice (as a staff a department) in comparison to the decision making role of the line departments.

As a result the heads of the personnel departments do not enjoy the same status as that of the other heads. Further the functioning of the personnel executives being confined within the organisation, they do not have any direct contact with the larger society. As such the profession does not enjoy the same status as that of other professions like Law, Medicine etc.

Regarding the formation and continuance of the professional organisation, the achievements of the profession is noteworthy. Both the professional bodies (IIPM and NILM) have emerged earlier to the management association (AIMA). In later years these two professional bodies have merged thereby strengthening the professional base of the personnel. Unlike medicine and law the entry into the personnel profession is not accredited by the professional body. The organisation, however, through its code of ethics regulates the activities of its members, it also publishes periodicals and other professional literature and organises seminars, conferences for the enrichment of the profession.

Thus, on the whole the personnel as a profession has achieved some noteworthy changes with regard to its discipline base, training and professional organisation. But with regard to its position both inside and outside the organisation and identification through its nomenclature, the profession still needs improvement.

ANNEXURE I

WELFARE OFFICERS (RECRUITMENT AND CONDITIONS OF SERVICE)

central model rules commitee's suggestions, 1957 variations in state rules

Number of Welfare Officers

Central Model Rule 3	The occupier of every factory where five hundred or more workers are ordinarily employed shall appoint at least one Welfare Officer; provided that where the number of workers exceed two thousand, one Welfare Officer shall be appoint for every two thousand workers or a fraction thereof.
Committee's Suggestion	There should be one Welfare Officer for factories employing between 500 to 2000 workers. Where the number of workers exceeded 2000, there should be an additional Welfare Officer for every additional two thousand workers or fraction thereof over 500. Where there were more than one Welfare Officer, one of them should be called the Chief Welfare Officer and the others Assistant Welfare Officers.
State Rules	State Rules in most cases follow the Model, but in Kerala it is laid down that one Woman Welfare officer should be employed where 300 or more women

are engaged. In Bihar, the Rules Provide as follows:

No. of Workers	*No. and Grade of Welfare Officers*
500–1000	1 (Grade III)
1001–1500	1 (Grade II)
1501–2500	2 (1 Grade I and 1 any other Grade)
2501–4000	3 (1 Grade I, 1 Grade II and 1 Grade III)
4001–6000	4 (1 Grade I, 1 Grade II and 2 Grade III)
6001–8000	5 (1 Grade I, Grade II, 2 Grade III and 1 Selection Grade)
8001–11000	7 (1 Selection Grade and 2 each of other Grades)
11001 and above	One additional Welfare Officer of any grade for every 2000 workers in excess of 11000 workers.

Under the Mines Rules, the question of appointing an additional Welfare Officer arises when the number of persons employed exceeds 2500 but for the employment of every additional 2000 workers or part thereof, extra additional Welfare officers are to be appointed.

Although provided under the Plantations Act, Government has so far not given effect to the clause on appointment of welfare officers in the plantations.

Qualifications

Central Model Rule 4

A person shall not be eligible for appointment as a Welfare Officer, unless he:

(a) Possesses a degree of a university recognised by the State Government in this behalf;

(b) has obtained a Degree or Diploma in Social Science from any institution recognised by the State Government in this behalf; and

(c) has adequate knowledge of the language spoken by the majority of the workers in the factory to which he is to be attached.

Provided that, in the case of a person who is acting

as a Welfare Officer at the commencement of these rules, the State Government may, subject to such conditions as it may specify, relax all or any of the aforesaid qualifications.

Committee's suggestion

It was agreed that the Welfare Officer should have a university degree and know the language spoken by a majority of the workers, but in view of the limited facilities for training in certain regions, the requirement of a degree or diploma in social science should have provision for relaxation. Preference could be given to those with a diploma.

State Rules

The U.P. Rules have two further limiting conditions, namely that the person appointed as a Welfare Officer must be domiciled in U.P. and must not be less than twenty-five years and not more than thirty-five years of age on appointment. Madras requires only a degree of a university in the State or Diploma from an institute recognised by the State Government.

Bihar Rules provide that a person shall not be eligible for appointment as Welfare Officer unless he has, inter alia, "qualified at a viva-voce test conducted by the Labour Commissioner, Bihar". Several States specify in their Rules the diplomas which are acceptable.

Committee's suggestion

The Central Government should consider drawing up a list of institutions whose diplomas would be recognised by all States, to enable Welfare Officers to be transferred from one State to another.

Recruitment of Welfare Officers

Central Model Rule 5

(1) The post of a Welfare Officer shall be advertised in all the prominent newspapers of the State.

(2) The selection shall be made from among the

	candidates applying for the post by a Committee appointed by the occupier of the Factory.
	(3) The appointment when made shall be notified by the occupier to the State Government or such authority as the State Government may specify for the purpose, giving full details of the qualifications, etc. of the officer appointed and the conditions of his service.
Committee's Amendment	The post shall be advertised in two newspapers having a wide circulation in the State, one of which should be an English newspaper.
State Rules	West Bengal Rules prescribe that the post of Welfare Officer may be filled by a person recommended by the Employment Exchange or the Appointments and Information Board of the Calcutta University, or by advertising in local papers.

Conditions or service of Welfare Officers

Central Model Rule 6	(1) A Welfare Officer shall be given appropriate status corresponding to the status of the other executive heads of the factory.
	(2) The conditions of service of a Welfare Officer shall be the same as of other members of the staff of corresponding status in the factory; provided that, in the case of discharge or dismissal, the Welfare Officer shall have a right of appeal to the State Government whose decision thereon shall be final and binding upon the occupier.
Committee's comment	One of the conditions of service is that in the case of discharge or dismissal, the Welfare Officer shall have a right of appeal to the State Government. It was considered that there should be no provision for such

appeal. If a Welfare Officer was dismissed by the employer and subsequently reinstated by the orders of Government, it was doubtful if he would be able to function effectively thereafter. One view was that following the Bombay practices, the employer should be required to consult the competent authority appointed by the State Government: before discharge or dismissal of a Welfare Officer. The need for such consultation will prevent employers from resorting to hasty or unfair dismissals, while still leaving the ultimate decision with the employer. Another view was that mere consultation with competent authority was not sufficient safeguard for the independent functioning of the Welfare Officer, but prior approval of competent authority should be prescribed. On the question whether there should be prior approval or only the obligation to consult before dismissed or discharge there was no unanimity of opinion in the Committee.

State Rules

Kerala and the Mines Rules merely contain the following: "The conditions of service of a welfare officer shall be the same as of other members of the staff of corresponding status". U.P. Rules lay down that "the welfare officer shall be subordinate to the General Manager of the factory and work under his direct control", and "shall have the status of an officer of the factory and shall be governed by the same rules in regard to dearness allowance, bonus, provident fund, leave, housing, medical and other facilities as are applicable to officer of similar status and grade in the factory".

West Bengal Rules state that the welfare officer "shall be subject to the terms and conditions normally applicable to the other officers of the factory and to the discipline laid down by the factory for its other officers", and that "no penalty should be imposed on him unless he has been first informed in writing of the grounds on which it is proposed to take action and has been afforded an adequate opportunity of defending himself; provided that if the management terminates the service of a welfare officer otherwise than under the terms of his contract, the reasons for the termination of service shall be reported to the State Government".

Bombay Rules provide that the employer before taking action to dismiss or discharge a Welfare Officer shall place the nature of the proposed action before the Commissioner of Labour, who may, after enquiry as he deems fit, advise the employer on the proposed action.

Bihar Rules decare that "no welfare officer shall be discharged, dismissed or otherwise punished except with the previous approval of the Labour Commissioner. Bihar, obtained on proceedings drawn up against the officer".

U.P. Rules go further and lay down that management shall not impose any punishment other than censure on a Welfare Officer except with the previous concurrence of the Labour Commissioner, who shall give the Welfare Officer an opportunity to explain the circumstances and if necessary, hear him in person.

Under the Mines Rules, it is obligatory for the owner, agent or manager to consult the Chief Inspector or an Inspector authorised by him in this behalf, before discharging or dismissing a Welfare Officer.

Pay Scales

The Central Model Rules do not lay down pay scales, leaving in to the status clause to achieve adequate remuneration for Welfare Officer. Government Labour Officers (Central Pool) Rules lay down a scale of Rs. 275-25-500-EB-30-650-EB-30-800.

State Rules

Kerala lays down a scale of not less than 200-10-240 EB-15-300. Under the Bihar the pay scales are as follows:

Grade III	–250–20–450
Grade II	–275–25–500–35–850–50–900
Grade I	–500–50–1000-EB–50–1200
Selection Grade	–1300–50–1800

Committee's comment

Opinion in the committee was divided; one view was that the Rules should not lay down any pay scales; another that only a minimum of Rs. 200 should be laid down, making it "clear that this should not tend to become the maximum".

Duties of Welfare Officer

Central Model Rule 7

The duties of Welfare Officer shall be:

(i) to establish contacts and hold consultations with a view to maintaining harmonious relations between the factory management and workers;

(ii) to bring to the notice of the factory management the grievances of workers, individual as well as collective with a view to securing their expeditious redress and to act as a negotiating officer with trade unions;

(iii) to study and understand the point of view of labour in order to help factory management to shape and formulate labour polices and to interpret these policies to the workers, in language they can understand;

(iv) to watch industrial relations with a view to using

his influence in the event of a dispute between the factory management and workers and to help to bring about a settlement by persuasive effort;

(v) to deal with wage and employment matters by joint consultations with the factory management and workers, representative bodies;

(vi) to exercise a restraining influence over workers going on illegal strikes and over management declaring illegal lockouts and to help to preventing anti-social activities;

(vii) to maintain a neutral attitude during legal strikes or lockouts and to help in bringing about a peaceful settlement;

(viii) to ensure fulfilment on part of the factory management of obligations statutory or otherwise, concerning the application of provisions of the Factories Act, 1948, and the rules made thereunder, and to establish liaison with the factory Inspector and the Medical Service concerning medical examination of employees, health records, supervision and hazardous jobs, sick visiting and convalescence, accident prevention and supervision of safety committees, systematic plant inspection, safety, education, investigation of accidents maternity benefits and workmen's compensation;

(ix) to promote relations between factory management and workers which will ensure productive efficiency as well as amelioration in the working conditions and to help workers to adjust and adapt themselves to their working environments;

(x) to encourage the formation of Works and Joint Production Committees, Co-operative Societies and Safety-First and Welfare Committees, and to supervise their work;

(xi) to ensure provision of amenities, such as canteens, shelters for rest, creches, adequate latrine facilities, drinking water, sickness and benevolent scheme payments, pension and superannuation funds, gratuity payments, granting of loans and level advice to workers;

(xii) to help the factory management in regulating the grant of leave with wages and explain to the workers the provisions relating to leave with wages and other leave privileges and to guide to workers in the matter of submission of application for grant of leave for regulating authorised absence;

(xiii) to secure welfare provisions, such as housing facilities, foodstuffs, social and recreational facilities, sanitation, advice on individual personal problems and education of children;

(xiv) to advise the factory management on questions relating to training of new starters, apprentices, workers on transfer and promotion, instructors and supervisors, supervision and control of notice board and information bulletins; to further education of workers and to encourage their attendance at Technical Institutes;

(xv) to suggest measures which will serve to raise the standard of living of workers and in general promote their well-being.

Committee's amendments

ii) The words "act as a liaison officer between management and labour" should replace the words "act as a negotiating officer with trade unions".

v) (vi) and (vii) Should be deleted as they are not appropriate function of a Welfare Officer.

viii) "To advise on fulfilment by the concerned departments of the factory" should replace the words " to ensure fulfilment on the part of the factory management".

ix) "To promote relations between the concerned departments of the factory and workers which will bring about productive efficiency" should replace to words "to promote relations between factory management and workers which will bring about productive efficiency", since the Welfare Officer would be dealing with heads of departments concerned.

xi) "to encourage" should replace "to ensure".

xiii) "to advise on provisions of welfare facilities" should replace "to secure welfare provisions".

State Rules

There is a fair amount of variation in the wording of Rule 7 in the various States. Some Rules omit certain parts of the Model Rules, others make changes in the wording. In the Kerala Rules the last part of subsection (vi) is changed to read; "help to bring about a settlement by persuasive efforts and to watch the working of collective agreements and the enforcements of industrial awards". Kerala has also added the study of absenteeism and labour turnover as one of the duties of the Welfare Officer. Bihar has added the duty of detecting and checking bribery and corruption and bringing such cases to the notice of the manager. Madras Rules omit the first part of (iii).

Rules 73(2) and 73(3) of the Mines Rules run as follows:

> 73(2) Notwithstanding anything contained in sub-rule (1), no Welfare Officer shall deal with any disciplinary case against a person employed in a mine, or appear before a Conciliation Officer, Court or Tribunal or behalf of the management . . . against a person or persons employed in the mine, except when he is re-

quired by the Conciliation Officer, Court or Tribunal to appear as an independent witness.

73(3) Every Welfare Officer shall keep a record of his day-to-day work and shall, at the end of every year, forward to the Chief Inspector through the manager of the mine concerned, a summary of the report of his work during the year.

Powers of Exemption

Model Rule 8 The State Government may, by notification in the official gazette exempt any factory or class or description of factories from the operation of all or any of the provisions of these Rules subject to compliance with such alternative arrangements as may be approved.

Women Welfare Officer

The Committee made the further recommendation that "where there was a large number of women workers, it was desirable that women welfare officers should be appointed".

See also note about Kerala under Rule 3 above.

ANNEXURE II

ILLUSTRATIVE LIST OF PERIODICALS IN PERSONNEL/ INDUSTRIAL RELATIONS PUBLISHED IN INDIA

1. Academy of Management Review.
2. Alternative.
3. ASCI Journal of Management.
4. Bombay Labour Journal.
5. Business India.
6. Capital.
7. Decision.
8. Economic Times.
9. Employee Relations.
10. Excellence in Supervision.
11. Growth.
12. Indian Administrative and Management Review.
13. Indian Journal of Applied Psychology.
14. Indian Journal of Commerce.
15. Indian Journal of Industrial Relations.
16. Indian Journal of Labour Economics.
17. Indian Journal of Public Administration.
18. Indian Journal of Social Work.
19. Indian Journal of Training & Development.
20. Indian Labour Year Book.
21. Indian Labour Journal.
22. Indian Management.
23. Indian Worker.
24. Industrial Engineering and Management.

25. Industrial Labour Relations Review.
26. Industrial Relations.
27. Industrial Relations News & Views.
28. Integrated Management.
29. Journal of Social and Economic Studies.
30. Labour Law Journal.
31. Lok Udyog.
32. Manager.
33. Management in Government.
34. Management Labour Studies.
35. Management Perspective.
36. Management Review.
37. Manpower Journal.
38. National Labour Institute Bulletin.
39. Organisational Dynamics.
40. Personnel Review.
41. Personnel To-day.
42. Prerana.
43. Productivity.
44. Social Welfare
45. Survey.
46. Vikalpa.
47. Yojana.

REFERENCES

1. *The Samaj*, dated 26.4.1990.
2. Organised Sector comprises of all establishments in the public sector and those non-agricultural establishments in the private sector employing 10 or more persons. Governments of India, *Economic Survey—1988-89,* New Delhi, Ministry of Finance, 1990, p. 62.

3. Besides apprenticeship and vocational training programme, the Ministry of Labour organised training programmes for craftsmen. A total of 1447 Industrial Training Institutes/Centres located in different parts of the country train craftsmen in Engineering and non-Engineering trades. See, Government of India, *Proformance Budget*, 1987-88, New Delhi, Ministry of Labour, p.44.
4. R.C. Saxena, *Labour Problems and Social Welfare*, Meerut, K. Nath & Co., 1986, pp. 900–902.
5. The result of such migration is the creation of the cities like Bombay, Madras, Calcutta, Ahmedabad, Hyderabad, Bangalore, etc.
6. K.N. Vaid, *Papers on Absenteeism*, New Delhi, Asia Publishing House, 1967, pp. 68–69.
7. AITUC (All India Trade Union Congress) was the first central federation started in 1920 followed by INTUC. (Indian National Trade Union Congress) in 1947, UTUC (United Trade Union Congress) in 1948 and HMS (Hind Mazdoor Sabha) in 1948.
8. The Trade Union Act, 1926, which permits any 7 workers to form a Union is also considered responsible for such multiplicity.
9. The Section 22 of Trade Union Act, 1926 is again held responsible for the phenomenon because it provides scope for outside leadership.
10. The observation made by Justice Shah of Bombay High Court evidently subscribes to this contention. See, Y.K. Tiwari, Trade Union in India, Changes and accountability in J.C. Rastogi, P.P. Arya and S.D. Tripathy (Eds.), *Planning for Industrial Relations Management—A 21st Century Perspective*, New Delhi, Deep and Deep Publications, 1987, pp. 156–169.
11. Baldev. R. Sharma, *The Indian Industrial Workers*, Delhi, Vikas Publishing House, 1974, p. 126.
12. N.R. Seth, "Trade Unions in an Indian Factory : A Sociological Analysis "*The Economic Weekly*, Vol. XII, No. 29 and 30, July 23rd, 1960, p. 1163.
13. E.A. Ramaswamy, *Industry and Labour : An Introduction*, Delhi, Oxford University Press, 1981, p. 120.

14. K.N. Subramaniam, *Labour Management Relations in India*, New Delhi, Asia Publishing House, 1967, p. 457.

15. The Union recognition is incorporated in some state laws like Bombay Industrial Relations Act and those of Madhya Pradesh and Rajasthan. The Code of Discipline provides for a criterial of recognition, but for its voluntary nature, its adoption is partial.

16. The percentage of lock out to the total disputes which was 8.62 (117 out of 1357) in 1961 increased to 23.78 (376 out of 1581) in 1986. Source : Labour Bureau, Simla.

17. Section 49 of Factories Act, 1948, section 58 of the Mines Act provide appointment of Welfare Officers if the number of workers employed are 500 or more. On the other hand, section 18 of the Plantation Labour Act, 1951 provides appointment of Welfare Officers in plantations employing 300 or more workers.

18. For details see Annexure-I.

19. As mentioned in the last chapter the linguistic facility has been recommended as a qualification for the labour officer. The same has been reiterated here.

20. K.N. Vaid, *Labour Welfare in India*, New Delhi, Shri Rama Centre for Industrial Relations & Human Resources, 1970, p. 342.

21. This is for the reason that social science include psychology, economics, political science, sociology, anthropology, history and also social work. M.V. Moorthy, *Principles of Labour Welfare*, Visakhapatnam, Gupta Brothers, 1968. p. 167.

22. Moorthy, *Principles*, p. 346.

23. Moorthy, *Principles*, p. 171.

24. C.A. Mayers and S. Kannappan, *Industrial Relations in India*, Bombay, Asia Publishing House, 1970, p. 255.

25. R.S. Kamat, "How Personnel Management can be more Dynamic?", *Capital*, Vol. 12, 1970, pp. 823-824.

26. For details see, Vaid, *Labour*, pp. 331-353.

27. S.K. Roy, *Mar. ıgement in India : New Perspectives*, Meerut, Meenakshi Prakashan, 1974, pp. 43-44.

28. Iswar Dayal, "Role of Personnel in Organisation", *Indian Journal of Industrial Relations*, Vol. 5, No. 3, January, 1970, p. 367.
29. Jacob, *Personnel*, p. 141.
30. Patro, *Human Resources*, p. 243.
31. Government of India, *Report of National Commission on Labour*, New Delhi, Ministry of Labour, 1969, p. 120.
32. Hon'ble Sri S.C. Shah, opening session, "All India Conference of Labour and Welfare Officer", *Social Science Journal*, Vol. XIV, 1953-54, p. 18.
33. The Royal Commission on Labour, in its Report recognises the prevalence of the Personnel Officers in Railways. See the report : Pages 139 and 164. Rustam S. Davar, however claims that the first Personnel Officer was appointed in a chemical concern in Bombay in 1951 with the regular personnel management functions as we understand them today being assigned to him. See, R.S. Davar, *Personnel Management and Industrial Relations in India*, New Delhi, Vikas Publishing House Pvt. Ltd., 1976, p. 38.
34. Kudchedkar, *Aspects of Personnel*, p. 66.
35. The relevance of social work is considered more in Indian Industrial set up than the other industrially developed countries, because of the primacy of welfare component in personnel management.
36. The branch of knowledge and techniques which concentrated on solving problems in a industrial set up was known as industrial social work which was changed to 'personnel social work' by the Zurich Study group in 1957, See for details Kudchedkar, *Aspects of Personnel*, p. 50.
37. Kudchedkar, *Aspect of Personnel*, p. 53.
38. N.K. Sethi, *Mangement Perspectives*, Bombay, Progressive Corporation Pvt. Ltd., 1972, pp. 109-110.
39. F. Harbison and C.A. Myers, *Management in the Industrial World : An International Analysis*, New York, McGraw Hill Book Company, Inc., 1959;

    Lambert, *Workers*.

Morris, *The Emergence.*

Sharma, *The Indian.*

N.R. Seth, *The Social Framework of an Indian Factory*, Bombay, Oxford University Press, 1968.

Roy and Menon (eds.), *Motivation.*

40. H. C. Ganguli, *Structure and Process of Organisation*, Bombay, Asia Publishing House, 1964; *Industrial Productivity and Motivation*, Bombay, Asia Publishing House, 1961.

D. Sinha, *Psychological Studies*, Patna, Patna Institute of Psychological Research and Service, Patna University, 1958.

P.R. Poduval, Organisational Effectiveness : A Systems Perspective in Roy and Menon (Eds.), *Motivation*, pp. 227-236.

Girishbala Mohanty, *A Text Book of Industrial and Organisatinal Psychology*, New Delhi, Oxford and IBH Publishing Co., 1983.

41. J.B.P. Sinha, The Psycho Social Background and Work Motivation, in Roy and Menon (eds.), *Motivation*, pp. 1–28.

Seth, *The Social.*

B.S. Baviskar, *The Politics of Development, Sugar Co-operative in Rural Maharashtra*, Delhi, Oxford University Press, 1971.

E.A. Ramaswamy, *The Worker and His Union : A Study in South India*, Bombay, Allied Publishers, 1977.

42. B.S. Murty, *Profiles of Indian Trade Unions (A Study in Orissa)*, Delhi, B.R. Publishing Corporation, 1986.

R.K. Das, *Collective Bargaining in India*, New Delhi, Discovery Publishing House, 1988.

Mohapatra and Patro, *Managing*.

K.C. Alexander, *Participative Management, The Indian Experience*, New Delhi, Sri Ram Centre for Industrial Relations and Human Resources, 1972.

B.P. Rath, *Industrial Relations and Participative Management*, New Delhi, Deep & Deep Publications, 1989.

V.G. Mhetras, *Labour Participation in Management : An Experiment in Induatrial Democracy in India*, Bombay, Manaktalas, 1966.

43. Arun Monappa and M.S. Saiyadin, *Personnel Management*, New Delhi, Tata McGraw Hill Publishing Company, 1979;

    Chatterjee, *Management*.

    Davar, *Personnel Management*.

44. Annexure-II is given at the end of this chapter.
45. Patro, *Human Resources*, p. 39.
46. S.D. Punekar, "The Personnel Manager in India", *Industrial Relations*, Vol. XXV, No. 2, March–April, 1973, p. 60.
47. McFarland, *Personnel*, pp. 81–82.
48. For details see, Patro, *Human Resources*, p. 39–63.
49. It was in 1985, that the then Prime Minister, Rajiv Gandhi included a separate Ministry of Human Resources Development combining the Ministries of Education, Cultural Affairs, Employment etc. under one banner.
50. R.D. Agarwal, *Dynamics of Personnel Management in India—A Book of Readings*, Bombay, Tata McGraw Hill Publishing Co. Ltd., 1973, p. 17.
51. Beach, *Personnel*, p. 77.
52. Flippo, *Principles*, p. 8.
53. W.D. Scott & R.C. Clothier, *Personnel Management*, New York, McGraw Hill, 1941, p. 20.
54. Ernest Dale, *Organisation*, Bombay, D.B. Taraporevala & Sons, 1975, p. 61; H. Koontz and C.O'Donell, *Essentials of Management*, New Delhi, Tata McGraw Hill Publishing Co. Ltd., 1978, p. 219.
55. L.A. Appley, *Management in Action : The Art of Getting Things Done Through People*, Bombay, The Times of India Press, 1965, p. 323.
56. Dale, *Organisation*, p. 67
57. Jacob, *Personnel Management*, pp. 139–141.

58.. Roy, *Management*, pp. 43–44

59. Dayal, *Role of*, p. 368.

60. Billimoria, *The Future*, Panakal, et al (eds.), *Readings*.

61. R.S. Pande, "The position and Responsibilities of the Personnel Department within an Undertaking in India", *Labour Management Series*, 7, Geneva, International Labour Organisation, 1960, p. 119.

62. Agarwal, *Dynamic Personnel*, p. 19.

63. Chatterjee, *Management of*, pp. 55–56 and 65.

64. M.N. Rudrabasavaraj, *Personnel Administration Practices in India*, Pune, Vaikuntha Mehta National Institute of Co-operative Management, 1969, p. 466.

65. Agarwal, *Dynamic Personnel*, p. 18.

66. Mary Sur (Ed.), *Personnel Management*, p. 73.

67. Roy, *Management*, pp. 44 and 51.

68. Jacob, *Personnel*, p. 142.

69. Dayal, *Role of*, p. 376.

70. Chatterjee, *Management of*, p. 56.

71. Jacob, *Personnel*, p. 142.

72. Tripathy, *Personnel*, p. 27.

73. Amitai, Etzioni., *Modern Organisations*, New Delhi, Prentice Hall of India (Pvt.) Ltd., 1965.

74. Harbison & Myers, *Management* in, p. 142.

75. For some time there was also an All India Council of Labour and Welfare Officers, as a sequel to the institution of Welfare Officers under the provisions of Factories Act. However, this council could not make much headway.

76. For details see report and Accounts of NIPM, 1987–88.

4

Current Status of Personnel Profession in India : Results of the Opinion Survey

Introduction

The previous two chapters traced the genesis of personnel profession in pre-independent India and outlined the current status of the profession in post-independent India respectively. Both these chapters have resorted to the historical approach and have recorded those events and developments which had an influence on the emergence and growth of personnel profession in India. Even though, objectivity is the strength of the findings of the previous two chapters; yet, the subjective opinions of all those who are involved directly or indirectly in the making of the profession are of equal importance in understanding and analysing the status of personnel profession currently. This chapter addresses itself to this objective.

Modus operandi of the Opinion Survey

Coverage and Tools of Data Collection

The survey covers institutes which are devoted to the training in personnel management; industrial organizations which employ the personnel executives; the trade unions and above all the practising personnel executives. Pre-designed mailed questionnaires (See appendices at the end of the report) were administered to the sample respondents under various categories. The study, due to its all-India coverage, justifies the use of mailed questionnaire as the tool of data collection.

Sampling Design

A list containing 31 institutes devoted to the training in personnel management was prepared[1]. (See Annexure-I at the end of the Chapter). It can be noted that, the list encompasses Social Work Institutes, Management Institutes and typical Labour and Personnel Management Departments mostly in Universities. All the 31 institutes were contacted, out of which 11 responded to the mailed questionnaire. Thus, around one third of the institutes responded. One institute (i.e, Sri Padmavati Mahila Viswavidyalayam, Tirupati) out of the eleven informed that, it has only social work specialisation and does not have personnel management as a special paper. Thus, only 10 respondents to the questionnaire (N=10) were considered under this category. However, the data collected and tabulated from these ten institutes were further augmented by information sent by 7 institutes (list given in Annexure II at the end of the chapter) as a response to the request made by the Post-Graduate Department of Industrial Relations and Personnel Management, Berhampur University. (It was necessary for updating the course structure). The Department at Berhampur University under whose aegis this study is being conducted is also included in the sample. Thus the data reported in this section reflected the course structure, nature of the degree awarded, teaching methods, etc. of 18 institutes of India.

In total 49 questionnaires were mailed to the corporate office of industrial organizations of which 35 were of the list of institutional members of NIPM. Attention was given to the choice of public and private sector organisations. (The list is given in Annexure-III at the end of the Chapter). Only on organisation i.e., Union Carbide responded. Despite Repeated reminders, no further response could be received. In order to compensate the data gaps caused by such poor response from industrial organisations, advertisements seeking personnel professionals were content analysed. A total of 375 advertisements collected from leading Newspapers in India during 1974-89 were subjected to such analysis. The advertisements were mostly analysed to know the qualification prescribed, job descriptions and specifications of the personnel professionals.

In order to elicit the opinion of unions on the general status of the personnel profession, central trade unions belonging to different ideologies and party affiliations were contacted. The questionnaires were sent in the personnel address of the leaders of these unions (see Annexure IV at the end of the Chapter). Despite several reminders the response received was only from four unions namely the AITUC, INTUC, CITU and BMS. Considering that these responses represent almost all the major central trade union federations, the data was interpreted.

In order to get the opinion of the personnel executives on an all India basis, the names and the mailing addresses of all the members of the NIPM were collected from the NIPM head office at Calcutta. As on February, 1988 there were 6521 members (inclusive of life, corporate and associate members only) spread over 38 branches including the headquarters. The institutional and student members have been excluded from the sample as personnel executives alone are taken as the respondents. From each branch around 1C per cent of the members were selected on a random basis (Refer Table 4.1).

Table 4.1 : Sample Design for Personnel Executives

S. No.	*Branch*	*Total Members Enrolled*	*Sample Size*	*Questionnaires returned undelivered*	*Total no. of responses received*	*Response rate in %age*
1	2	3	4	5	6	7
	Eastern Region					
1.	Asansol	104	11	--	2	
2.	Assam	45	4	--	1	
3.	Bihar	162	19	--	8	
4.	Bokaro Steel City	84	8	--	3	
5.	Calcutta	898	92	3	22	

(Contd.)

Table 4.1 : (Contd.)

1	2	3	4	5	6	7
6.	Dhanbad	56	5	--	3	
7.	Durgapur	60	6	1	3	
8.	Patna	97	10	2	4	
9.	Ranchi	154	12	--	4	
		1660	167	6	50	31.05
	Western Region					
10.	Ahmedabad	118	10	--	5	
11.	Baroda	97	9	--	3	
12.	Bombay	759	71	6	13	
13.	Goa	82	7	--	2	
14.	Nasik	79	10	2	4	
15.	Pune	75	8	--	1	
		1210	115	8	28	26.16
	Central Region					
16.	Andhra Pradesh	267	29	2	10	
17.	Bhillai	114	9	--	4	
18.	Godavari	46	6	1	2	
19.	Nagpur	57	6	--	2	
20.	Orissa	86	17	1	9	
21.	Utkal	77	12	--	6	
22.	Visakha	102	9	1	4	
		749	88	5	37	44.57
	Northern Region					
23.	Allahabad	92	10	--	2	
24.	Delhi	399	41	1	13	
25.	Haryana	66	6	--	2	
26.	Jaipur	66	6	--	3	

(Contd.)

Table 4.1 : (Contd.)

1	2	3	4	5	6	7
27.	Punjab	73	7	--	3	
28.	Rajasthan	75	9	1	3	
29.	Uttar Pradesh	235	31	1	8	
		1006	110	3	34	31.77
	Southern Region					
30.	Coimbatore	77	7	1	5	
31.	Karnataka	558	58	5	25	
32.	Kerala	214	26	2	15	
33.	Madras	494	55	3	16	
34.	Mysore	86	9	1	4	
35.	Trivandrum	109	13	--	5	
36.	Madurai	73	9	3	4	
37.	Tiruchy	127	16	--	8	
		1738	193	15	82	46.06
	Head Quarters					
38.	Headquarters	158	11	--	5	45.45
	Total	**6521**	**684**	**37**	**236**	**36.47**
39.	Ex-students of the Dept. who were not in the rolls of NIPM	38	38	--	19	50.00
		6559	**722**	**37**	**255**	**37.22**

Source : Compiled from the data collected.

A total of 684 questionnaires were mailed of which 37 returned up-delivered. Out of the remaining 647 questionnaires, 236 field-in questionnaires were received. Out of those 236 questionnaires, 150 were received within a few days after the questionnaires were mailed, while 48 were received after sending the first reminder, 25 after second reminder and only 13 after the third and the final reminder. In addition to the NIPM members, 38 questionnaires were mailed to ex-students of the IRPM Department,

Berhampur University who were not members of NIPM. From these 29 filled in questionnaires were received. Thus altogether 255 filled in questionnaires were received, and the information given through these questionnaires was analysed. The population considered for the study was 6559 personnel executive, out of which 722 got included in the sample, thereby amounting to 11 per cent sample rate. The 255 responses account for 37.22 per cent response rate. However, taking the total responses as a percent value of the population, the sample rate comes to 3.9 per cent. The sample rate though appears to be small; yet, it adequately represents the different types of organisations, sectors and occupational levels. (Refer Tables 4.2, 4.3 and 4.4).

Table 4.2 : Organisationwise Distribution of the Personnel Executives

S.No.	*Name of the Organisation*	*No. of Personnel Executives*
1.	Factory	183
2.	Mines	18
3.	Dock and Ports	2
4.	Railways	4
5.	Banking	10
6.	Airlines	1
7.	Plantations	1
8.	Any other*	36
	Total	**255**

* Includes organisations like electricity board, marketing, railways etc.

Source : Compiled from the data collected.

Table 4.3 : Sectorwise Distribution of Personnel Executives

S.No.	*Name of the Sectors*	*No. of Personnel Executives*
1.	Public Sector	126
2.	Private Sector	110
3.	Corporations	8
4.	Government Departments	8
5.	Cooperatives	3
	Total	**255**

Source : Compiled from the data collected.

Table 4.4 : Occupationwise Distribution of Personnel Executives

S.No.	*Occupation Level*	*No. of Personnel Executives*
1.	Top Management	57
2.	Middle Management	157
3.	Lower Management	41
	Total	**255**

Source : Compiled from the data collected.

Justification of the Questionnaire Design and Framework of Analysis

Though separate questionnaires were designed for various categories of respondents; yet, they were meant to serve a common purpose and to arrive at integrated results. All the questionnaires refer to the status of personnel profession in India, though they differ with regard to the thrust.

The questionnaire for educational institutions was devoted to the training of personnel professionals, and the role of these institutes in the following areas of enriching the personnel discipline and profession:

— keeping abreast with the development in personnel management and initiating concomitant changes in nomenclature, syllabus, format of the degree, teaching technology;

— Teaching methods resorted;

— Initiative taken by the academic institutes to develop interaction between the theory and practice through consultancy, research and mutual sharing of ideas and problems between the professionals and academicians;

— Enriching the personnel discipline through professional literature;

— Providing the right type and quality of personnel professionals at the right time to the organisations by employment information and placement programmes.

The questionnaire to the industrial organisations, was designed to elicit the following informations:

— Specific functions that are assigned to the personnel professionals, their relationship with the line managers and other staff executives;

— Training needs of fresh personnel professionals turned out by institutes and universities.

— Possibility of standardization of job descriptions and specification for personnel professional.

— Initiative taken by the organisation to have mutual interaction with academics in terms of research, consultancy, etc.

The questions asked to the trade unions mostly centered round the issues like:

— The role of the personnel department in resolving disputes and maintaining harmonious relations between the management and union.

— Role of the personnel department as a problem solving machinery for cases of grievance, indiscipline, and other individual problems of workers.

— The way the personnel department is used in organisations.

— Personality vis-a-vis training in making effective personnel executives.

— The need for statutory welfare officer in the light of the role of the union in collective bargaining.

The questionnaire administered on the personnel executive sought to get the information on the following aspects:

— The type of exposure the professionals have acquired in terms of subjects studied, teaching methods received and the overall quality of the degree attained and the extent to which these are adequate for their effective functioning.

— The day-to-day activities carried out by them either as main or subsidiary function in the personnel administration, industrial relations, welfare and miscellaneous areas.

— The attitude of the top management, line departments, workers and unions towards the personnel functionaries.

— The attitude of the top management, line departments, workers and unions towards the personnel functionaires.

— The factors that contribute in securing employment and promotion of personnel executives.

— The institute of welfare office vis-a-vis the status of personnel profession.

— Personnel department's strategy in line-staff relation.

— The nature and quality of personnel job in organisations.

The information sought through the questionnaires administered to the four different categories of respondents, when viewed in he light of theoretical framework and conceptual design framed in the first chapter relating to the features of a profession, indicate that the respondents are made to render their opinion on the extent to which the personnel function in organisations has qualified to be considered a profession. In this context, the responses would be broadly analysed under the following heads irrespective of the category of respondents.

— Job title, responsibilities and functions.

— Job specifications and training base.

— Disciplinary base of the profession.

— The status and role of personnel executives vis-a-vis the top management, line executives, unions and workers.

— Role of NIPM as a professional body in enriching the profession.

The core issues identified above not only represent the gist of information collected and collated from all the categories of respondents; but also cover the important factors that contribute towards the enrichment of any profession.

Job Title, Responsibilities and Functions

Profession is identified by its nomenclature. Medicine, Law, Engineering, Teaching, etc. are professions which are universally denoted by a specific nomenclature. And the person practising the profession is recognised by the designation that goes with the nomenclature such as doctor, engineer law year/advocate, teacher, etc. In this regard to what extent the profession of managing people at work has acquired a common nomenclature thereby assigning a common designation to the professionals is first attempted.

For this, the information collected from the advertisements and personnel executives have been analysed. The nomenclature with which the advertisements have been made, the real designations of personnel executives and the designation that they would prefer these three formed the basis of analysis. The Table 4.5 which incorporates and presents all the three data is self explanatory.

Table 4.5 : The Designation Prevailing and Expected by the Personnel Executives

Designation	*Extent of prevalence as indicated by the advertisements* (N=375)	*Extent of Prevalance as indicated by the actual designations of the* (N = 255)	*Expected Designation by the presonnel Executives* (N = 221)*
Personnel	182 (48.53)	174 (68.24)	131 (59.28)
Industrial Relations	24 (6.40)	13 (5.10)	7 (3.17)
Labour	10 (2.67)	5 (1.96)	------
Welfare	21 (5.60)	3 (1.18)	1 (0.45)
Administrative	5 (1.33)	-------	1 (0.45)
Human Resources	36 (9.60)	11 (4.31)	56 (25.34)
Combination of any of the above	97 (25.87)	49 (19.21)	19 (8.60)
Employee Relations	------	------	6 (2.71)
Total	**375**	**255**	**221**

* Only 221 out of the 255 respondents have responded their choice for the question.
Source : Compiled from the data collected.

From among the 375 advertisements collated, around 48.53 per cent account for the 'Personnel' nomenclature, followed by combined nomenclature (25.87 percent) wherein more than two designations are clubbed together. 'Industrial relations' and 'administration' are the most frequent combinations with 'personnel'. 'Human Resources' nomenclature has accounted for 9.6 per cent of nomenclature and 'welfare' nomenclature despite its statutory base account for only 5.6 per cent.

In reality, 'Personnel' designation dominates as evident from the fact that 68.24 per cent of the responding officers possess this designation. Same as the trend in advertisements, the combined designations which account for 19.21 per cent, is the next in order. While pure 'administration' designation draws a blank, 'welfare' accounts for only 1.18 per cent. The 'Human Resources' designation has already gained currency as 4.31 per cent have got it, while 'industrial relations' account for 5.1 per cent of designations.

'Personnel' (59.28 per cent) retains the status of most sought after designation. And contrary to the trends in advertisement and real designations, the combined designation is sought only by 8.6 per cent whereas the 'human resources' designation is preferred by 25.34 per cent of the respondents. 'Welfare' designation is virtually shunned as only one respondent preferred it.

From the above account, the following trends can drawn:

— 'Personnel' is the most popular nomenclature.

— 'Labour' and 'Welfare' designations are least preferred and prevailing.

— 'Combined ' designations dominated by 'Personnel' and appended by either 'Industrial Relations' or 'Administration' is largely prevailing out lowly preferred.

— 'Human Resources' is gaining currency as a nomenclature and it is also greatly preferred.

The responsibilities assigned to the personnel professionals was sought from the corporate office of various industrial organisations. The reasons was highly discouraging as only one out of 49 organisations responded to the questionnaire. The lone organisation i.e., the Union Carbide India Limited held that the personnel executives are assigned functions connected with staff, industrial relations and human resources development. It, further observed that, it is difficult to have a uniform job description for this function in all organisations. This contention demands attention as it is believed that with a variety of nomenclatures and designations sometimes describing functional specializations and sometimes hierarchal positions, the personnel responsibility is bound to defy uniform job description. In order to further establish this, the job description data collected from 375 advertisements for personnel executives of which 201 have categorically mentioned about the specific job description have been analysed form the data shown in Table 4.6. The analysis adopts the categorization made by Dalton E. McFarland dividing all the responsibilities into three categories namely, Integrated, Split Function and Extended[2].

It is evident from the table that 141 (70.15 per cent) job descriptions come under split function, followed by 32 (15.92 per cent) under integrated and 28 (13.93 per cent) under extended categories. The personnel designation dominates in all the three categories. Combined designations find the second place. It is pertinent to observe that, the split-function responsibilities mostly bifurcate rather than trifurcate. Combination of personnel and labour welfare responsibilities together and separating industrial

Table 4.6 : Functional Responsibility of Personnel Executives

Functional Category	*Responsibilities*	*No. of Advts.*	*Percentage*
Integrated	Personnel	29	15.92
	Combination of any other	3	
Split function	Personnel	79	
	Industrial Relations	11	
	Labour	4	
	Welfare	8	70.15
	Administration	1	
	Human Resources	5	
	Combination of any other	33	
Extended	Personnel	10	
	Industrial Relations	1	
	Administration	2	13.93
	Combination	15	
Total		**201**	

Source : Compiled from the data collected.

relations is a popular trend. The extraneous functions which are assigned to the personnel under extended responsibilities include estate, medical, security, public relations, community services, stores, telecommunications, township, transport, general administration etc., over and above the three core responsibilities. These trends coverage upon to establish the contention that the personnel profession is still in a restless search for an identity because neither it is known by a common nomenclature nor does it have defined boundaries of functional responsibilities.

In this context, the functions actually performed by the responding personnel executives is analysed so as to know the reality. The 36 functions enlisted under those performed by the executives are divided into four groups namely, personnel administration, industrial relations, labour welfare and miscellaneous, each consisting of nine functions. The executives were required to indicate whether they are performing the functions or not and if performing, whether it is their primary or subsidiary function. The response of the executives who indicated that they are performing the personnel administration, industrial relations, labour welfare and miscellaneous functions is tabulated and presented in Tables 4.7, 4.8, 4.9 and 4.10

Table 4.7 : Personnel Functions Performed by Personnel Executives

Sl. No.	*Functions*	*Performing as*	
		Main	*Subsidiary*
1.	Advising and influencing the formulation of personnel policy and procedures	131	77
2.	Job Analysis and Job Evaluation	42	81
3.	Recruitment, Selection and Induction of Workers	150	58
4.	Recruitment, Selection and Induction of Executives	88	57
5.	Wage and Salary Administration	111	72
6.	Performance Appraisal	143	77
7.	Employee Training	99	86
8.	Career Planning and Promotion	101	77
9.	Managing communication through brochures, notices, handouts, pamphlets, office administration etc.	122	69
	Mean	109.67	72.67
	C.V.	29.82	13.57

Source : Compiled from the data collected.

Table 4.8 : Industrial Relations Functions performed by personnel executives

Sl. No.	Functions	Performing as Main	Performing as Subsidiary
1.	Grievance Handling	186	46
2.	Disciplinary action i.e. charge-sheeting and punishment	169	49
3.	Conducting Domestic Enquiry	115	54
4.	Negotiation with union/workers' representatives	178	50
5.	Work of Labour Courts, Conciliation etc. on behalf of the Management	139	67
6.	Assisting in prohibition of unfair labour practices	87	74
7.	Taking initiative to maintain cordial Labour-Management Relations	187	45
8.	Fostering Participative Management	126	73
9.	Preparing briefs and reports on disputes for the management	143	55
	Mean	147.77	57.00
	C.V.	23.57	19.96

Source : Compiled from the data collected.

Table 4.9 : Labour Welfare Functions performed by personnel executives

Sl. No.	Functions	Performed as Main	Performed as Subsidiary
1.	Administration of statutory health, welfare and safety provisions	103	82
2.	Canteen Management	102	66
3.	Organising recreational, cultural, education and medical programmes	83	87
4.	Looking after housing, labour colony and welfare centre	70	56
5.	Administering social security provisions	96	80
6.	Time office, personnel records, statistics on labour turnover and absenteeism	140	51
7.	Conducting studies and research on labour problems	41	66
8.	Sanctioning leave, loan and advances etc.	127	77
9.	Employee counselling	134	80
	Mean	99.55	71.66
	C.V.	32.12	17.40

Source : Compiled from the data collected.

Table 4.10 : Miscellaneous Functions performed by personnel executives

Sl. No.	*Functions*	*Performed as*	
		Main	*Subsidiary*
1.	Administering suggestion schemes	72	77
2.	Looking after security, watch and ward	70	47
3.	Public relations, liaison and news bulletin etc.	75	61
4.	Sending reports and returns to Govt. Deptt.	143	68
5.	Guiding students of personnel Management/ Industrial Relations/Labour Welfare/Social work in their field work	87	93
6.	Receiving and entertaining visitors	75	101
7.	Going round the work	99	96
8.	Conducting Exit Interview	71	65
9.	Attending to odd jobs at the request of the Management	66	135
	Mean	84.22	82.55
	C.V.	28.81	32.22

Source : Compiled from the data collected.

respectively.

From the tables it can be interpreted that industrial relations function is performed either as a main or subsidiary function on an average by 82.83 per cent (highest among all the categories of functions) of the executives. The same figures for personnel, labour welfare and miscellaneous functions are 73.19 percent, 68.67 per cent and 67.37 per cent respectively. It is also evident from the data presented in the tables that industrial relations function is performed by majority of the executives (72.16 per cent of the respondents who perform this function) as a primary function. The personnel function stands next with 60.15 per cent of the executives as a main function. This is being followed by labour welfare and miscellaneous functions with 58.14 per cent and 50.5 per cent respectively.

The industrial relations function not only scores over the others as a main function but also is the most consistent function as the value of coefficient of variation is the least (23.57). Next in the order is the miscellaneous function with coefficient of variation with 28.81 followed by personnel (29.82) and labour welfare (32.12).

As a subsidiary function, however, the miscellaneous category dominates with 49.50 per cent on an average performing it. Labour welfare function comes next with 41.86 percent followed by personnel management with 39.85 per cent and industrial relations with 27.84 per cent. As a subsidiary function the personnel function is the most consistent one with coefficient of variation value at 13.57 and the miscellaneous function the least consistent one (C.V. value 32.22). In between these two lie the labour welfare function (17.40) and industrial relation function (19.96).

Thus the analysis of the data relating to the functions actually performed by the personnel executives indicate that all the four different functions are performed in different degrees. While the industrial relations emerge as primary functional responsibility the miscellaneous function stands mostly as a subsidiary function. In between these two lie the personnel and labour welfare functions.

In the light of the data relating to job title, it can be interpreted that despite the predominance of personnel nomenclature, the industrial relations function becomes the major activity. However, combined responsibilities integrating two or more functions together characterize the functions really performed by the personnel executives. Some non personnel activities become equally main and subsidiary responsibilities thereby providing an extended nature to personnel function.

Job Specifications and training Base

It has been observed that having a uniform job description for the dynamic personnel profession is quite difficult. Nomenclatures differ, job demands and responsibilities too differ. Depending on the status of the personnel executives in the hierarchy, they might perform either decision-making role or executive role. In this context, the notion that the personnel profession could have a generalized job specification so as to serve two co-equal purposes namely.

i) To integrate the specifications with the job description date thereby knowing what the company expects from the training schools and institutes turning out personnel executives; and

ii) to study the efficacy of the training base in responding to the company expectations.

These two purposes are served by interpreting the data collected from four sources namely the personnel executives. Academic institutes, advertisements and corporate industrial organisations.

The educational qualifications preferred by different organisations from prospective candidates seeking entry into the personnel profession has been collected from the advertisements and the data thus collected is presented in Table 4.11.

Table 4.11 : Job Specifications Collected from Advertisements

S.No.	*Qualifications Prescribed*	*Number*
1.	Degree and/or Diplomas in Personnel Management/ Industrial Relations/Labour Welfare/Labour Legislation	234
2.	Degree in Management and Business Administration	101
3.	Degree in Behavioural Sciences	07
4.	Degree in Social Work	48
5.	Degree in Social Welfare	27
6.	Degree and/or Diploma in Social Science	46
7.	Degree in Public Administration	06
8.	Diploma from Indian Society of Training and Development	03
9.	Degree in Human Resources Development	03
10.	Degree in Law (Additional Qualification preferred)	102
11.	No specific qualification yet demanding work experience	18

Source : Compiled from the Advertisements collected.

It is evident from the table that a degree or diploma in personnel and other related disciplines like Industrial Relations, labour Welfare and Labour Law is the qualification specified by the organisations followed by a Degree in MBA. A degree in Law is preferred mostly as an additional qualification. Relating this finding with the nomenclature and designation of posts advertised in personnel area (Table 4.5), it can be inferred that, as majority of posts do have Personnel designation, logically they require degree in Personnel management. Another important revelation is that Social Work degree is preferred only by 48 advertisements while a degree in Social Sciences is preferred by 46 advertisements and degree in Social Welfare is preferred by 27 advertisements. These qualifications are mostly in consonance with the requirements under the law for the post of Welfare Officers. Peculiarly degree in Behavioural Sciences, Human Resource

Development are witnessed in advertisements though there is no evidence of such degrees being awarded in India. Rather they become a part and parcel of the course curricula. It is to be noted that, the advertisements mostly demand more than one qualification as alternatives. All these tend to subscribe to the contention that the job specification as evident from the prescribed qualifications is gradually pruning down to the specialisation of personnel management.

The observations made by the Union Carbide, the lone respondent from the category of corporate offices, reads that, "Personnel function is highly professionalised and therefore general management training in itself cannot equip them sufficiently to be effective on the job". This contention advocates in favour of personnel specialisation as against a degree in business management. The 101 advertisements with specifications of M.B.A. degree as against the 234 advertisements with personnel specialisation further substantiates this contention. Around 18 advertisements have not specified any qualifications, yet demand work experience. This information need to be analysed in the light of the practice in some organisations where non-qualified people are employed at junior positions in the personnel departments and over years rise in the hierarchy to hold senior positions. Even after so much of growth in the academic institutions and towards professionalisation of personnel management, the continuity of this short of non-professional practice need to be viewed with concern.

As against the expectations of the employing organisations, what really is the qualification of the practising personnel professionals and which qualification is adequate, was sought from the personnel executives. The data in this regard is presented in Tables 4.12 and 4.13 respectively.

The Table 4.12 provides the professional qualification of the personnel executives with the year of passing. The table indicates that as many as 92 (36.95 per cent) respondents have either two years degree or diploma in personnel management/ industrial relations. This subscribes to the finding made relating to job specification prescribed by the industrial organisations, where degree-diploma in personnel management/industrial relations is the most required qualification for the personnel executives. Also it corroborates the findings made relating to job title where the personnel is the most used designation and the job descriptions of the personnel executives where the personnel/industrial relations are the

Table 4.12 : Professional Qualification of the Personnel Executives and year of passing

S. No.	Qualifications of the Personnel Executives	1955–59	1960–64	1965–69	1970–74	1975–80	1980–	Total responding Executives
1.	Two Year Degree/Diploma in Personnel Management/Industrial Relations/Labour Welfare	4	12	9	18	27	22	92 (36.95)
2.	MBA degree with specialisation in Personnel Mgt.	--	--	3	2	6	7	18 (7.23)
3.	Degree in Social work with specialisation in Personnel Management/Labour Welfare/Industrial Relations	4	5	7	9	9	8	42 (16.87)
4.	Degree in Social work without specialisation in Personnel Management/Labour Welfare/Industrial Relations	--	1	1	3	--	--	5 (2.00)
5.	Two years diploma in Social work/Social Service with specialisation in Personnel Mgt.	--	1	2	3	5	7	18 (7.23)
6.	6 months–1 year Diploma in Personnel Mgt./Industrial Relation/Labour Welfare/Social work etc.	2	6	3	10	14	22	57 (22.90)
7.	Degree/Diploma in Social Science with specialisation	--	2	--	1	--	--	3 (1.20)
8.	Degree/Diploma in Social Science without specialisation	--	--	--	1	3	2	6 (2.41)
9.	Degree in Law/Engineering	--	5	1	--	1	1	8 (3.21)
	Total							**249(100.00)**

Figures in the parantheses indicate per cent value.

Source : Compiled from the data collected.

dominant functions.

The diploma holders in personnel management/ industrial relations who account for 22.90 per cent indicate that a number of executives have joined the profession without any professional qualification and have acquired the diplomas latter. M.B.A. degree holders, whose number is only 18 (7.23%), show that their entry into the profession is not very encouraging.

The Table 4.13 presents the data regarding the adequacy of different qualifications for the personnel profession. From the table it is evident that majority of the respondents (200) feel that a two years degree in Personnel Management/ Industrial Relations is fully adequate followed by MBA degree with specialization in personnel management (138) and Social Work degree with personnel management as specialisation (92). It can be seen that a degree in social work, without specialisation in personnel management/industrial relations are held to be inadequate for the profession by 168 respondents. A sizeable (157) respondents felt that the six months to one year diploma in labour welfare, personnel management and labour law is inadequate for the profession. From the above account, it can be inferred that the personnel executives perform specialised functions in the areas of personnel administration, industrial relations and labour

Table 4.13 : Professional Qualification Preferred by the responding executives (N = 255)

Course	*Fully Adequate*	*Partially Adequate*	*Inadequate*
2 years degree course in Personnel Management/ Industrial Relations/Labour Welfare/Labour Legislation.	200	43	3
2 years MBA degree with specialisation in Personnel Management	138	89	15
2 years degree in Social work with specialisation in Personnel Management	92	129	18
2 years degree in Social work without specialisation	14	53	168
6 months to 1 year diploma in Labour Welfare/ Personnel Management/Labour Legislation	14	71	157

Source : Compiled from the data collected.

welfare. And in order to perform them they need to be specially trained. Generalists and persons with flair for social work are not competent to meet the growing complexities of personnel profession. Further, the direct recruitees without qualification who legitimize their entry by short duration diploma courses are also considered inadequately prepared for the growing challenges of the profession.

With these findings in view the training base provided to the personnel executives is now attempted for analysis. In order to do this, the content analysis of the courses taught by different academic institutions turning out personnel executives, the courses actually read by the responding personnel executives and the teaching methods adopted by the institutions and received by the executives become the basis of analysis.

The institutions devoted to the teaching of personnel management, industrial relations and other related subjects can be trifurcated into the following categories.

(1) Those which award degree or diploma in either Personnel Management (PM) or Industrial Relations (IR) or Labour Welfare (LW) and/or in their combinations.

(2) Those which are pure social work institutions having special papers in Personnel management and Industrial Relations (PM & IR).

(3) Those Business Management Institutions awarding M.B.A. degree with Personnel Management as a special appear.

The course content of 29 institutes in these categories are presented in Table 4.14, 4.15 and 4.16. The analysis of the course content of the institutions providing degree or diploma in Personnel Management and Industrial Relations indicates that though there is no uniformity; yet, the subjects like Personnel management, Industrial Relations, Organisational Behaviour, Labour Legislation, Labour Welfare etc. are offered as compulsory papers. They have provisions for block field-work but some of them also provided concurrent field work Specific aspects of industrial relations and personnel management such as collective bargaining, participative management, manpower planning, training and development, comparative trade unionism, etc. are offered as special papers from which a student has to elect subject/s of his own choice. Much similar to the compulsory papers there is absence of any uniformity in the list of subjects of special papers (Table 4.14).

The syllabi of the Social Work institutes reveal that they give major emphasis to the various subjects related to Social Work. However, Personnel Management, Labour Welfare, Labour Legislations, and Industrial Relations are offered as elective subjects in majority of the Social Work Institutes. Personnel Management is offered as a compulsory paper only in two Social Work Institutes while Industrial Relations is offered by one institute only. (Table 4.15). The analysis of the course content offered by the institutes awarding M.B.A. degree reveals that these institutes offer teaching programme in various fields of management like Finance, Marketing, Production, Materials, System, etc. including Personnel. Majority of the institutes cover Personnel Management, Industrial Relations and Organisational Behaviour as compulsory papers because Human Resources Management is considered to be an important input to every field for management. In addition some institutes provide specialisation in the filed of personnel and industrial relations (Table 4.16).

In the light of the findings made above, the courses actually studied by the personnel executives sought in the questionnaire are analysed. Not only that the executives were required to indicate whether they have studied the 13 identified courses, but also they had to specify the degree of usefulness of the course in their day-to-day work. For the later purpose a three-point scale consisting of most, moderate and less useful categories has been designed. The responses elicited are presented in Table 4.17.

The subjects of personnel management, labour legislation, trade unions and industrial relations, labour welfare administration, labour economics and labour problems, industrial psychology, sociology and organisational behaviour and project report are studied by almost all the respondents. Around 60 per cent of the executives have studied such subjects like general management, social work, social research and have undertaken field work. It is pertinent to observe that the responding executives exposed to computer courses account for a negligible 12.16 per cent. This finding when corroborated with the findings relating to the course content of the institutes reveals that, it is only few MBA Departments who provide computer courses and the finding that fewer number

Table 4.14 : Subjects taught by Industrial Relations and Personnel Management Institutes

Name of the Institutes	*SUBJECTS OFFERED*													
	1	2	3	4	5	6	7	8	9	10	11	12	13	14
Department of Industrial Relations and Personnel Management, Andhra Uni.		C	C	C	C	C			C		C	C	C	
Department of Personnel Management and Labour Welfare, Utkal University	C	C	EC	C	C	C		C	C		C	C	C	
Department of Personnel Management, Xavier Institutes of Social Science, Ranchi	C	C		C	C	C		C	C	C			C	C
National Institute of Personnel Management by Correspondence Course, Calcutta	C	C	C	C		C			C					
Department of Personnel Management by Correspondence Course, Annamalai Uni.		C	C	C					C					
Department of Industrial Relations and Personnel Management, Berhampur Uni.	C	C	C	C	C				C		C		C	
Department of industrial Relations, Mysore University			C						C					
Department of Personnel Management and Labour Welfare, Kurukshetra University	C	C	C		C		C		C		C	C	C	
Department of Labour and Social Welfare, Patna University		C	C		C		C				C	C	E	
Department of Industrial Relations, XLRI, Jamshedpur.		C	C	C	C	C		C					C	
Department of Personnel Management and Industrial Relations, Tata Institute of Social Science, Bombay.		C	C	C	C		C		C			C		

1. General management 2. Personnel Management/Human Resources Management. 3. Industrial Relations 4. Organisational Behaviour 5. Labour Legislation 6. Social Research and Quantitative Techniques 7. Industrial Psychology 8. Industrial Sociology 9. Labour Welfare & Social Security 10. Computer Training 11. Project Work/Field Work/Dissertation 12. Viva-Voce 13. Industrial and Labour Economics 14. Social Work

Note : C and E indicate Compulsory and Elective respectivey. *Sources* : Compiled from the course of studies of different institutes and University Depts.

Table 4.15 : Subjects taught by Social Work Institutes offering Personnel Management, Industrial Relations and Labour Welfare papers

Name of the Institutes	SUBJECTS OFFERED													
	1	2	3	4	5	6	7	8	9	10	11	12	13	14
Department of Social Work, University of Delhi						C			C		C			C
Department of Social Work, Jamia Millia Islamia University, Delhi		C	C		C				C		C			C
Dept. of Social Work, Visva Bharati		E	E			C					C	C		C
Department of Social Work, (Labour Welfare), Indian Institute of Social Welfare and Business Management, Calcutta		C			C		C				C	C		
Department of Social Work, Udaipur School of Social Work, Udaipur.		E				C			E		C	C		C
Department of Social Work, Kashividyapith			E			C			E		C	C		C
Social Work, NISWAS,Bhubaneswar.						C			E		C	C		C

1. General management 2. Personnel Management/Human Resources Management. 3. Industrial Relations 4. Organisational Behaviour 5. Labour Legislation 6. Social Research and Quantitative Techniques 7. Industrial Psychology 8. Industrial Sociology 9. Labour Welfare & Social Security 10. Computer Training 11. Project Work/Field Work/Dissertation 12. Viva-Voce 13. Industrial and Labour Economics 14. Social Work

Note : C and E indicate Compulsory and Elective respectivey. *Sources* : Compiled from the course of studies of different institutes and University Depts.

Table 4.16 : Subjects taught by Management Institutes offering papers in Personnel Management, Industrial Relations and Labour Welfare

Name of the Institutes	*SUBJECTS OFFERED*													
	1	2	3	4	5	6	7	8	9	10	11	12	13	14
Indian Institue of Management (IIM), Lucknow.	C	CE Adva-nced	CE Comp-ulsory	C		C				C	C			
Indian Institute of Management (IIM), Bangalore.	C	C	C	C						C	C		—	
Indian Institute of Management (IIM), Ahmedabad	C	C	C	C						C	C			
Dept. of M.B.A. School of Management Studies, Cochin University.	C	C	C	C										
Dept. of M.B.A., Institute of Social Welfare and Business Management Calcutta	C	CE		C		C	E			C				
Dept. of M.B.A., M.L.N. Institute of Research and Business Administration, University of Allahabad	C	C		C										
Dept. of M.B.A., South Gujarat Uni.	C	C	C	C										
Dept. of M.B.A., Punjabi University	C		C		C		C		C					
Dept. of M.B.A., Uni. of Madras	C	C	C	C										
Dept. of M.B.A., Faculty of Management Studies, University of Delhi.	C	CE Advanced	E		E									
Dept. of M.B.A., B.K. School of Management, Gujarat University	C	C	C	C		C								

1. General management 2. Personnel Management/Human Resources Management. 3. Industrial Relations 4. Organisational Behaviour 5. Labour Legislation 6. Social Research and Quantitative Techniques 7. Industrial Psychology 8. Industrial Sociology 9. Labour Welfare & Social Security 10. Computer Training 11. Project Work/Field Work/Dissertation 12. Viva-Voce 13. Industrial and Labour Economics 14. Social Work

Note : C and E indicate Compulsory and Elective respectively. *Sources* : Compiled from the course of studies of different institutes and University Depts.

Table 4.17 : Subjects studied by the personnel executives

Subject	*Whether Studied*		*If yes, the extent of its use in day-to-day activities*		
	Yes	*No*	*Most useful*	*Moderately useful*	*Least useful*
General Management	156	91	81	71	4
Personnel Management	243	10	202	39	2
Labour Legislation	245	7	207	36	2
Trade Unionism and Industrial Relations	244	7	172	63	9
Labour Welfare Administration	239	15	133	86	20
Labour Economics and Labour Problems	221	28	72	111	38
Industrial Psychology, Sociology and Organisational Behaviour	234	19	138	81	15
Methods and Fields of Social work	163	88	40	71	52
Social Research Methods	158	91	30	78	50
Field Work (Concurrent)	148	97	55	62	31
Field Work (Block)	129	119	53	49	27
Project Report/Dissertation	210	37	75	84	51
Computer Course	31	212	13	12	6

Source : Compiled from the data collected.

of MBA degree holders are entering into the personnel profession justifies the lack of computer training with the personnel executives. However, there has been a greater agreement with the trend that the computers are increasingly in use in personnel functions thereby requiring a retraining of personnel executives in Personnel Information System. This is substantiated by the 73 per cent (185 out of 255) of Personnel Executives agreeing to this contention. Thus the executives are found to be mostly exposed to training in personnel management, industrial relations, and other related subjects. Taking into account the job description and specification profile as portrayed in previous discussion, it can be inferred that the personnel profession is greatly demanding specialised knowledge and to this extent the executives are properly equipped with theoretical knowledge.

Some important findings can be made by analysing the response to the extent of utility of the subjects in the day-to-day work of the executives. Personnel management and labour legislations are the two subjects which are found to be most useful in the day-to-day activities of around 80 per cent of the personnel executives. Whereas industrial relations, labour welfare, organisational behaviour are considered most useful by around 50 per cent of the personnel executives. The finding that the subject of social work is only moderately useful confirms to the previous inference that the impact of social work on personnel profession is waning out. Similar trend with methods of social research also subscribes to the general contention that personnel profession in India is weak in the area of personnel research conducted by the professionals.

Contrary to the expectations the field work and project report (dissertation) which are meant to provide practical exposure to the executive are considered only moderately useful by the practitioners of the profession.

These findings, when viewed in the light of the analysis made of the course content of the academic institutes, prompt one to infer that, those institutes which provide full time courses in personnel management, labour legislation, industrial relations and other related subjects are better equipped to turn out practising professionals. The social work and MBA institutes are not fully competent to turn out the personnel professionals. This finding goes a long way in identifying personnel profession as independent of the general management profession.

The training process involves communication and learning. Efforts are always afoot to improve communication skills for better learning. In case of professional training, the teaching methods assume great importance because communication media for better learning involves learning by listening, learning by doing and learning by seeing, etc. In this regard what teaching methods are adopted by the academic institutions and to which of the methods the executives have been exposed and benefits accrued thereof have been elicited from the responding executives. The data collected from the responding executives and the academic institutes have been presented in Table 4.18 and Table 4.19 respectively.

Table 4.18 : Methods of Teaching Received by the Personnel Executives

Methods of Teaching	*Whether Received*		*If yes, the extent of its benefit for your profession*		
	Yes	*No*	*Most beneficial*	*Somewhat-beneficial*	*Least beneficial*
Lecture	241	7	142	92	7
Seminars & Conferences	194	52	140	54	--
Case Analysis	202	39	155	47	1
Role Playing and Simulation Exercises	146	96	97	40	9
Audio-visual Devices	99	142	57	37	5
Discussions and Games	170	71	115	52	3

Source : Compiled from the data collected.

From the Table 4.18 it can be seen that Lecture method is a very popular method of teaching as around 95 per cent have given an affirmative answer to this. The various participant methods of teaching such as seminar, case analysis, role playing, discussion and games is the next popular method as 57 per cent to 79 per cent of the respondents have held that they have been imparted training through these methods. Audio-visual method is the least common method of training as around 39 per cent of personnel executives only have expressed this method as being used in their training programmes. However, in terms of the extent of benefit of the different teaching methods in the profession the participant methods of teaching out-score the non-participant methods as around 68 to 77 per cent of the respondents who have received training through these methods found them as most beneficial.

The response of the training institutes with regard to the teaching methods they adopt while imparting training to the personnel executives show that lecturer, seminar and conferences, and case analysis are the most common methods followed bv discussion and games, role play, audio-

Table 4.19 : Teaching Methods Adopted by the Educational Institutions and their Extent of Use

Methods of Teaching	*Whether Adopted*		*If yes, the extent of its use*		
	Yes	*No*	*Always Used*	*Mostly Used*	*Seldom Used*
Lecture	10	--	7	3	--
Seminars & Conferences	9	1	1	3	5
Case Analysis	9	1	2	5	2
Role Playing and Simulation Exercises	6	4	1	3	2
Audio-visual Devices	6	4	2	4	--
Discussions and games	8	2	2	4	2
Computer Programming	6	4	1	4	1

Source : Compiled from the data collected.

visual devices and computer programming. So far as the extent of use of these methods, the lecture method scores out all other methods as majority of the institutes held it to be a regularly used method. In addition to the lecture method the institutions do also use the other participant methods of teaching. But probably these methods play a supportive role to the lecture method as their extent of use by the institutes is not as regular as the lecture method. Computer programming, which is mostly a latest addition in the training programmes of the personnel executives has not yet become a common method of teaching.

Disciplinary Base of the Personnel Profession

When theory is advanced by practice and practice is disciplined by theory, the resultant helps the process of improving both. And a profession in order to be perfected needs basically a strong disciplinary foundation. Developing tho discipline hence, is the joint responsibility of both the theoreticians and practitioners. The forums through which discipline can be enriched are research, consultancy and constant out turn of professional literature. In this part, the role played by the professionals, academic institutes and organisations in contributing to the enrichment of the discipline is projected. The informations sought from these respondents would obviously get related to the observations made in the Chapter-3 about the disciplinary base.

Keeping this as the objective, questions were asked to the personnel professionals, academic institutes and industrial organizations basically highlighting their role and the extent to which they interact with each other, thereby facilitating meaningful fusion between theory and practice in personnel management.

As regards the role of the personnel executives in enriching the personnel discipline, they were asked about the extent of participation in conferences, seminars and refresher courses and also the frequency of contributing research articles. The opinion collected on these two aspects are tabulated and presented in Table 4.20.

Table 4.20 : Frequency of Attending Conferences and Refresher Courses and Contributing Articles to Professional Journals in the Field of Personnel Management and Industrial Relations by the Personnel Executives

N = 255

	Frequently	*Sometimes*	*Rarely*	*Never*
Attending conferences and refresher courses	67 (26.27)	157 (61.57)	26 (10.19)	4 (1.57)
Contributing Articles	6 (2.35)	74 (29.22)	63 (24.71)	102 (40.00)

Source : Compiled from the data collected.

Figures in the parentheses indicate per cent value.

It can be seen from the table that a majority (87.84%) of the personnel executives either frequently or sometimes attend conferences and/or refresher courses. Thus to a lager extent the personnel executives attempt to keep themselves abreast with the development in the personnel discipline. On the other hand, their contribution in enriching the personnel literature is not very encouraging as a mere 2.35 percent of the executives contribute articles frequently and 29.02 per cent contribute only sometimes. But most surprising is the fact that 40 per cent of the executives as revealed by them never contribute any article. Of the 6 respondents who frequently contribute article, 3 are from the top management, 2 from middle management and 1 from the lower management. Their contribution of articles is mostly to the internal journals of the organisation, and sometimes to journals published outside the organisation.

In addition to the above, the personnel executives were asked whether they are performing personnel research as one of their functions to which 41.96% (107 out of 255) of executives have given an affirmative reply. Of these 107, while 41 executives held that it is their main function, 66 held that they perform it as a subsidiary function. Thus at the organisation level personnel research as one of the functions of the personnel executives has not yet been well established.

Personnel executives can involve themselves in personnel research for contributing to the development of the personnel discipline, if the industrial organisation in which they are employed provides them adequate opportunities. Hence, the role of industrial organisations is no less important than the personnel executives and the academic institutions. But, the response of the personnel executives shows that this aspect has been quite neglected by the industrial organisations as around 76 per cent (193 out of 255) of the executives agreed that "Personnel research at organisational level is not given adequate attention in India".

It was also tried to get the response directly form the industrial organisations with regard to their role in organising personnel research on their own or in assisting research projects undertaken by the academic institutions. As mentioned earlier, the Union Carbide was the only organisation is presented here. So far as initiating research activities on is own, the company held that, "there is hardly any research activity in this area in the company". However, in connection with assisting in the research projects on personnel management undertaken by academic institutes, the company held that it usually assists and extends cooperation in research projects undertaken by academic institutions. Thus the role of the industrial organisation is limited to extending co-operation only to the research activities initiated and organised by academic institutions.

The academic institutions were made to respond to such issues as research, consultancy, interaction between them and industrial organisations made by the department towards enriching the professional literature. From the responses, it could be seen that, the academic institutes have a luke-warm attitude to these issues. Excepting the Indian Institute of Management at Bangalore. Ahmedabad and Lucknow, none of the social work and personnel management departments have consultancy facilities in personnel areas. The procedural constraints prevailing in the Universities and institutes can be attributed for the absence of consultancy services in those academic institutions. The consultancy programmes undertaken by the IIMs reportedly help in the process of developing case studies for use as teaching aids. The same trend is also found in the area of publishing in-house journals as the IIMs are the only academic institutes who have their own publications.

With regard to the interaction between the academic institutes and the industrial organisations, the IIMs have greater interaction for placement services and employment. With regard to research and integration of theory and practices, these institutes do not give primary importance despite their infrastructural capabilities and greater patronage they receive from the industrial and other employing organisations. Thus, the role of these institutes is quite inadequate in enriching the professional status of personnel.

The social work institutes and those institutes imparting training in personnel and industrial relations do have interactions with industrial organizations only to the extent of field placements and to some extent employment. Research is not an important contact area between any of the academic institutes and business organisations. Though scholars conduct research in personnel area in industries, such research efforts are not supported by the organisations. Action research is a far cry where the organisations at the maximum acquit themselves from this responsibility by supplying half-baked and concocted data. The very response to the present study both from industrial organisations and academic institutes bear testimony to this finding. Thus, the academic institutes are neither fully oblivious of nor totally engrossed with industrial organisations. This luke-warm relatedness perhaps is the sole cause for the personnel academics' and professionals' failure to advance theories emanating from the typical organisational realities in India. This evidently subscribes to the dominance of western theories and western personnel literature in the course contents of the academic institutes. Thus, the discipline base of personnel profession is not that well founded so as to support the growth of a healthy profession.

Status and Role of Personnel Executives vis-a-vis Top Management, Line Executives, Unions

In this part the personnel executives are required to project a self image of their real role and status. For this purpose they were made to respond to broadly two questions. One indicated the level of satisfaction they have on the manner in which they are treated by the top and line executives, their colleagues and others. By seeking their level of agreement on 23 statements the questionnaire has attempted to elicit the image drawn by the personnel executives about the status of personnel profession.

On the other hand, the top management and unions have been asked to give their opinion about the working of the personnel department. This two-fold analysis of self-image and image profiled by others present a wholesome picture about the role and status of personnel executives.

The responding executives were required to record their level of satisfaction on, ten issues which are of vital importance for their functioning. There were four choices namely; fully satisfied, moderately satisfied, least satisfied and not satisfied, which have been assigned weightages of 4,3,2 and 1 respectively. After computing the overall scores under each statement, the number of no opinions have been substracted at the rate of one point for one no response. Thus, the final score has been computed keeping the total number of responses i.e., N at 255. The data thus computed is presented in Table 4.21.

The scorings have been analysed by placing them on the points continuum starting from 255 (supposing all respondents to be not satisfied with the ten issues) to 1020 (supposing all respondents to be fully satisfied). Between these two extreme score values three intermediate patterns indicating the values of 510 (for least satisfied) 765 (for moderately satisfied) and 892.5 the mid-way between high and moderate satisfaction so as to indicate the extent of satisfaction have been identified (Fig. 4.1).

The scores earned by the ten issues as indicated in column 8 of the Table 4.21 when distributed on this continuum indicate that, the respondents have mostly exhibited moderately satisfied opinion on the issues. It

Fig. 4.1

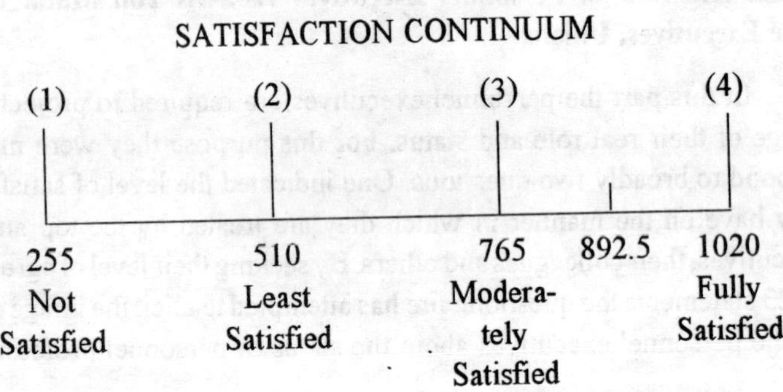

is only in case of the issue No. 9 which reads 'team spirit and cooperation of colleagues in your own department', that the respondents with a score of 893 have recorded opinion tilting marginally towards fully satisfied. With regard to the issue No. 10 which reads 'career advancement opportunities for personnel executives in your organisation', the respondents have recorded less than moderately satisfied score with 744.

From the interpretation of the coefficient of variation computed for the four levels of satisfaction, it can be concluded that the respondents are more consistent in their exhibition of moderately satisfied opinion. Whereas despite the low scoring in least satisfied and not satisfied responses, there is a great amount of inconsistency.

For further meaningful analysis, the ten issues are ranked basing on the score values secured by them (Col. 8 of Table 4.21). Considering the first five as top order ranks and the rest five as second order ranks, some important inferences can be made as under. The intra-departmental co-operation, managerial and line recognition given to personnel advice, inter departmental relations and worker's attitude towards the personnel functions have assumed high order ranks of one to five respectively. Whereas, the attitude of union on the personnel department, decision-making freedom enjoyed by the personnel department, conditions of employment, scalar position and career advancement opportunities of the personnel department have secured low order ranks from 6 to 10 respectively. It can be inferred that relations-oriented issues have gained higher scores which

Table 4.21 : Level of satisfaction indicated by the personnel executives regarding status in the organisations.

Variable	*Fully Satisfied*	*Moderately Satisfied*	*Least Satisfied*	*Not Satisfied*	*No Opinion*	*Total Score*	*Rank Awarded*
1. Consideration given by the Management to the advice and suggestions provided by the Personnel Department	448 (112)	381 (127)	22 (11)	0 (0)	–5 (5)	846	2
2. Importance given to the advice and guidance of the Personnel Department by the line personnel	448 (112)	345 (115)	34 (17)	5 (5)	–6 (6)	826	4
3. The attitude of the workers towards your Department as a whole.	396 (99)	399 (133)	24 (12)	5 (5)	–6 (6)	818	5
4. The attitude of the union and its leaders towards your department.	432 (108)	348 (116)	40 (20)	4 (4)	–7 (7)	817	6
5. Scalar position of your department in the organisational hierarchy.	408 (102)	327 (109)	46 (23)	5 (5)	–6 (6)	780	9
6. Decision making freedom and authority that your department enjoys with regard to personnel functions.	436 (109)	321 (107)	54 (27)	8 (8)	–4 (4)	815	7
7. Conditions of employment and work of the personnel executives in your organisation.	412 (103)	357 (119)	38 (19)	10 (10)	–4 (4)	813	8
8. Cooperation from other departments	388 (97)	411 (137)	34 (17)	3 (3)	–1 (1)	835	3
9. Team spirit and cooperation of colleagues in your own department.	668 (167)	213 (71)	18 (9)	1 (1)	–7 (7)	893	1
10. Career advancement opportunities for personnel executives in your organisation.	312 (78)	342 (114)	78 (39)	18 (18)	–6 (6)	744	10
C.V. =	**19.88**	**15.10**	**43.14**	**83.22**			

Source : Compiled from the data collected.

The figures in parenthesis indicate the number of responses (N).

means that personnel executives are more satisfied with their relationship with line colleagues, supervisors and workers; whereas they are not satisfied with their job content, job conditions and job offers. This is an important finding which negates the popular notion that the advice rendering job of the personnel executive is seldom liked by the top and line managers.

The reflexation on the lack of career advancements however, need to be interpreted as a condition caused by minimum availability of promotional avenues. Taking personnel as a specialised field of management, the fact that most personnel jobs become dead-end jobs, unless and otherwise hierarchical upward mobility opportunities are available appears justified. Further, the lack of career advancement opportunities can not be construed as a consequence of organisational politics, because majority of the personnel executives considered competence on the job, professional qualification and previous experience as the three important criteria for employment advancement. Whereas very few respondents gave credence to personnel contact, recommendations, caste and other such loyalties as criteria for career advancement. (Table 4.22).

Table 4.22 : Criteria held to be helpful for employment advancement by the Personnel Executives

Criteria	*Extent of Helpfulness*		
	Most Helpful	*Moderately Helpful*	*Least Helpful*
Professional Qualification	175	71	3
Competence on the job	214	30	6
Previous experience	166	80	3
Personal contact and recommendations	50	123	74
Caste, linguistic, regional and such considerations	14	78	154

Source : Compiled from the data collected.

The finding that unions' attitude towards the personnel department's role is not very encouraging, appears justified when related to the previous findings that industrial relations function dominates the activities of personnel department. In the industrial relations the union as the representative of the workers is an important actor as much as the personnel department as a representative of the management. The wrath and grouse that the union holds for the management undoubtedly will fall on the personnel department whose functions have been epitomized by such phrases as 'fire fighting' 'shock absorbing' etc. So it is but natural that, the personnel executives are less satisfied with the union. This finding however, can be tallied with the responses of the unions.

In order to gauge the opinions of the unions about the personnel function, a questionnaire embodying 12 statements was administered with the choice of a four point agreement scale namely, agree, partially agree, disagree and no opinion. Four National level trade unions responded to the questionnaire. The responses were weighted with 3 points for agree, 2 points for partially agree and 1 point for disagree. A negative point for no opinion was levied which was substracted form the total. The data thus computed is presented in Table 4.23.

The statements project a positive profile of the personnel function. When the respondents agree, they deem to have a fairly good opinion about the nature of personnel profession. Taking this analytical framework it can be observed that the opinion of the unions is largely negative as 7 out of 12 statements have secured values less than 8 (partially agree).

The statements, which secured values more than 8 i.e. denoting the opinion towards agree level, are about the importance given to the personnel department by the corporate authority in union management relations, the importance of personality factors and professional training in equipping the personnel executives to tackle the personnel job. The statement which received full agreement is that, "the personnel department is used as a protective shield by the line manages and the corporate authority against the onslaught of the unions". This denotes that the unions are sympathetic about the precarious condition in which the personnel executives find themselves.

The pseudo neutrality stance of the personnel department; its dubious role in ensuring prohibition of unfair labour practices; it being used by management to harass workers; and the unions' lack of faith in its performance are some opinions which come to the limelight. However, the

Table 4.23 : Trade Union Response on the Function of the Personnel Job N=4

S.No.	Statements	Agree	Partially agree	Disagree	No opinion	Total
1.	The personnel department remains neutral while mediating between the union and the management whenever there is dispute	–	–	3 (3)	–1 (1)	2
2.	The personnel department helps in maintaining harmonious union-management relations by ensuring equal implementation of unfair labour practices.	3 (1)	–	2 (2)	–1 (1)	4
3.	The personnel department is not used by the management against the interest of the workers.	–	–	4 (4)	–	4
4.	The Personnel department acts as a representative of the management while not antagonising the interest of the trade unions.	6 (2)	2 (1)	1 (1)	–	9
5.	The personnel department is not anti-union.	–	6 (3)	1 (1)	–	7
6.	The Personnel department is given all importance by the corporate authority in union-management relations.	6 (2)	4 (2)	–	–	10
7.	The Union has faith in personnel department as a problem solving machinery for cases of grievances, discipline, disputes, etc. involving workers interest.	–	–	4 (4)	–	4
8.	The personnel department has authority for granting concessions to workers.	3 (1)	2 (1)	2 (2)	–	7
9.	The personnel department is used as a protective shield by the line managers and the corporate authority against the onslaught of the unions.	12 (4)	–	–	–	12
10.	It is the personality of the personnel executives which determines the quality of the personnel profession.	6 (2)	4 (2)	–	–	10
11.	Professional training equips the personnel executives to tackle the personnel jobs.	9 (3)	2 (1)	–	–	11
12.	The statutory welfare officer is not necessary in view of the strength of the union in ensuring welfare measures through collective bargaining.	–	6 (3)	1 (1)	–	7

Source : Compiled from the data collected. *Note* :The figures in parenthesis indicate the number of responses.

anti-union stance of the personnel department, its concession-sanctioning authority are partially agreed. And contrary to the previous findings, the institution of Welfare Officer is not considered totally redundant. The personnel executives do not stand opposed to the unions' interest again is partially agreed.

Thus the overall profile of the personnel executives and their functions as perceived by the union is negative.

The twenty-three statements on which the responding executives gave their level of agreement has been analysed under three debatable aspects of the image of personnel profession namely (i) role and status of welfare officer vis-a-vis the profession, (ii) line-staff dynamics in personnel function; and (iii) inherent nature of the personnel job. The institution of Welfare Officer is statutory. It's working in reality contradicts the statutory expectations, thereby causing some curiosity and concern for personnel profession. In this context the personnel executives were required to indicate the level of agreement with the statements relating to the institution of Welfare Officer. The table 4.24 presents the data.

It is evident from the table that 71.38 per cent of the respondents have agreed to the contention that the management can make the position of welfare officer difficult, thereby making the statutory protection meaningless. Around 49 per cent of the respondents when agree to the suggestion that management should be given free hand to appoint welfare officers and to define their duties, compound the management's prerogative and denounces the statutory provisions which have not changed much since coming into force in 1951. The disagreement of 55.3 per cent of the respondents to the suggestion that the welfare officer should be appointed and paid by the Government subscribes to the contention that there should be no interference at all in the organisation and administration of the welfare function. To substantiate this stand, the level of agreement shown by 69.8% of the responding personnel executives to make the welfare offices a part of the management team but not a 'neutral' 'third force' goes a long way. Further, the welfare function is demanded by 46.67 percent of the responding executives to be given the status of a separate function. Thus, it can be inferred that the respondents have bitterly criticized the prevailing practices in organising the welfare function, and apparently

Table 4.24 : Level of Agreement of Personnel Executives Towards the Institution of Welfare Officer.

S.No.	*Statements*	*Level of Agreement*			
		Agree	*Partially agree*	*Dis-agree*	*No opinion*
1.	The statutory protection given to the welfare officer becomes meaningless if the management, the pay master makes the welfare officer's position difficult.	182 (71.38)	56 (21.96)	15 (5.88)	2 (0.78)
2.	The defined status, duties and conditions of appointment remaining unchanged make the institution of welfare officer redundant.	110 (43.14)	89 (32.90)	43 (16.86)	13 (5.10)
3.	Management should be given the freedom to appoint welfare officers and define their duties.	125 (49.02)	52 (20.39)	75 (29.41)	3 (1.18)
4.	The welfare officer should be fair to both sides out cannot and should not remain neutral.	175 (68.53)	43 (16.86)	31 (12.16)	6 (2.35)
5.	The welfare officer must be a part of the management team but not a third force.	178 (69.8)	40 (15.69)	35 (17.73)	2 (0.78)
6.	The welfare officer should be appointed and paid by Government.	81 (31.76)	30 (11.76)	141 (55.30)	3 (1.18)
7.	The welfare function should be given separate functional status alongwith personnel and industrial relations instead of clubbing them together.	119 (46.67)	37 (14.51)	94 (36.86)	5 (1.96)

Source : Compiled from the data collected. *Note* :The figures in parenthesis indicate the number of responses.

meant the following changes to be brought about—

i) The statutory status be deleted. Government interference of any kind be stopped.

ii) Management be given full freedom to appoint, define the duties and remunerate the Welfare Officers considering them as part of the management team.

iii) Welfare Officer be given independent status.

The staff role of the personnel department creates some typical problems and raises questions relating to the functional status of this department vis-a-vis the line executives. In this regard the personnel executives were required to respond to some questions on the line-staff dynamics. The data collected is presented in Table 4.25.

The line-staff dynamics is interpreted in terms of three dimensions, namely.

(1) Staff's (Personnel Executives) relationship with the line and strategies needed for maintaining the relations.

(2) Line's response to the staff advice; and

(3) Above all, the top management's strategy in ensuring line-staff amity.

All these converge upon warding off the potential conflict between the line and staff.

Decision making as a lien prerogative and assisting/advising as a staff responsibility mark their role authority. The responding personnel executives to the tune of 61.57% by agreeing with the advice and assistance role for the personnel department as against 55.3% seeking decision making powers vouch for the traditional staff role of personnel, Yet, it can be inferred that decision making powers in some personnel areas are sought by more and more number of personnel executives. When 74.12% of the responding personnel executives agree that the staff advice of personnel can be elevated to the level of control on line by virtue of its expertise nature and by suitably improving staff assistance to the level of specialised services, mean that, they prefer to retain their staff activity. The

Table 4.25 : Level of Agreement of Personnel Executives on Line and Staff Dynamics

S.No.	*Statements*	*Level of Agreement*			
		Agree	*Partially agree*	*Dis-agree*	*No opinion*
1.	The advisory and staff nature of personnel job is inadequate and hence should be assigned with decision making authority.	141 (55.3)	64 (25.09)	47 (18.43)	3 (1.18)
2.	The personnel department should depend more on informal and personal approach rather than on formal authority in relation to line and staff.	157 (61.57)	67 (26.27)	27 (10.59)	4 (1.57)
3.	The personnel executive should elevate his advisory position to the level of expertise so as to make the line dependent on the staff advice.	189 (74.12)	45 (17.65)	16 (6.27)	5 (1.96)
4.	The top management gives preferential treatment to the line executives over the personnel staff.	106 (41.56)	100 (39.22)	46 (18.04)	3 (1.18)
5.	The personnel executives are unable to project a worthwhile image thereby presenting a low profile of the profession.	66 (25.89)	102 (40.00)	85 (33.33)	2 (0.78)
6.	Some kind of orientation in the personnel job to line personnel would be helpful in bridging the gap between line and staff.	208 (81.57)	37 (14.51)	7 (2.74)	3 (1.18)
7.	Personnel Executives do not get the credit for the success in the organisation but only receive blames for the failures.	100 (39.22)	109 (42.75)	44 (17.25)	2 (0.78)
8.	Personality factors like intelligence, perseverence, art of listening, honesty, integrity, communication skill are highly essential for effective functioning of the Personnel Executives.	215 (84.32)	33 (12.94)	2 (0.78)	5 (1.96)

Source : Compiled from the data collected. *Note* :The figures in parenthesis indicate the number of responses.

expectation is that right advise and timely assistance rendered by the personnel executives can have the same effect of control on line.

For this, the personnel executives believed that they should depend on their human relations skill of persuasion and personal approach and by projecting a worthwhile image. The very fact that one fourth of the personnel executives have agreed and 40 per cent of them have partially agreed on the contention that, "the personnel executives are unable to project a worthwhile image thereby presenting a low profile of the profession", reveals that the personnel executives virtually blame themselves for the inadequacy of the staff role being appreciated and accepted by the line. Thus in a sort of self-introspection the personnel executives find inadequacies in their own performance rather than in the line command or top management's strategy in maintaining the line-staff amity. This finding can be further substantiated when 39.22 per cent of the respondents partially agree and 18.04 per cent of them disagree that, the top management gives preferential treatment to the line. It is only 41.56 per cent who agree with this contention. It can be interpreted that the top management's preferential treatment to the line will not interfere in the efficacy of the personnel staff.

However, a great majority of 81.57 per cent of the personnel executives agreed that an orientation programme for the line in staff role will improve the line-staff relations. Through role rotation and other such programmes the line can have a realistic feel of the staff job and that may lead to the proper comprehension, appreciation and acceptance of the staff role.

Over 80 per cent of the respondents either agree or partially agree on the statement that "personnel executives do not get the credit for the success in the organisation but only receive blames for the failures". It highlights in one way the contention that, machines and the line executives who are in the direct production line will be incapacitated only by the failure in human resources management. But, in reality the human resources management, i.e., 'getting things done through the efforts of others' is carried out by the line managers at the shop floor. And personnel executives only oversee the practices whether they are attuned with the company policies or not. However, the only reason why the personnel executives are looked down with suspicion as trouble shooters may be is their role which ordains them to deal with the unions. So, when organisation fails to achieve results, the tendency of all might be to blame the human factor. As a result, the line absolves its responsibility and accountability in human resources management when industrial relations problems occur. The 'watch dog' and 'police' role of the personnel executives and more so of the welfare officers bring the profession into disrepute. This is a reality which must be put up with by the personnel executives, because industrial relations in their dominant role.

One of the major findings drawn from the discussions made above is that, the personnel executives believe that they shall depend on their personal acumen of persuasiveness and not on any formal authority for effective interaction with the line. The very fact that 84.32 per cent of the respondents agree with the statement that "personality factors like intelligence, perseverance, art of listening, honesty, integrity, communication skill are highly essential for effective functioning of the personnel executive", further substantiates their belief.

Instead of searching for alibi in relationships with the line or in the attitude of the top management, the personnel functionaries need to search for their inherent nature of job vis-a-vis their functioning. This point emerges from the discussions made on line-staff dynamics. With regard to inherent nature of personnel job, the personnel executives were required to indicate their level of agreement with 8 statements. The data is presented in Table 4.26.

Industrial relations functions inclusive of union negotiation and collective bargaining; dealing with individual disputes arising out of disciplinary actions and grievances and collective disputes; are highly litigate prone. The statutes governing industrial relations may be the cause for such litigation. It has been found earlier that the industrial relations dominate the personnel function. Hence, there is every logic that the personnel job will be overtly legalistic in nature. Now that, 37.65 per cent of the personnel executives agree and 43.14 per cent of the partially agree with the legalistic nature of personnel job, reiterates this contention.

Ensuring human dignity, humanizing work, human relations etc., are considered to be one of the main areas of personnel job. Yet, 52.55 per

Table 4.26 : Level of agreement of personnel executives on the inherent nature of personnel job.

S.No.	*Statements*	*Level of Agreement*			
		Agree	*Partially agree*	*Dis-agree*	*No opinion*
1.	The personnel job is highly legalistic i.e., looking after litigations raised by Trade Unions, individual/collective disputes, disciplinary cases, grievances etc.	96 (37.65)	110 (43.14)	44 (17.25)	5 (1.96)
2.	The personnel job is only humanistic i.e., looking after the administration of welfare measures, counselling, motivation etc.	42 (16.47)	134 (52.55)	71 (27.84)	8 (3.14)
3.	The personnel job is running errands or doing odd jobs for the management.	30 (11.76)	54 (21.18)	168 (65.88)	3 (1.18)
4.	The personnel job is predominantly of fire fighting and shock absorbing nature in relation to the union.	74 (29.02)	106 (41.57)	72 (28.23)	3 (1.18)
5.	The personnel job is no better than a file clerk's job i.e., dealing with paper work only.	10 (3.92)	18 (7.06)	221 (86.67)	6 (2.35)
6.	The personnel job is highly challenging and respectable.	219 (85.89)	29 (11.37)	5 (1.96)	2 (0.78)
7.	Understanding, analysing, predicting and modifying human behaviour at work is the main task of the personnel executives.	203 (79.61)	49 (19.22)	2 (0.78)	1 (0.39)
8.	The confidence of the top management in the nature of personnel job ultimately decides the philosophy behind personnel job.	181 (70.98)	61 (23.92)	9 (3.53)	4 (1.57)

Source : Compiled from the data collected. *Note* :The figures in parenthesis indicate percent value.

cent of personnel executives partially agree and 27.84 per cent disagree with statement that 'the personnel job is only humanistic i.e., looking after the administration of welfare measures, counselling, motivation, etc. 'It is agree by 16.47 per cent of the respondents. The inference hence can be that, the humanistic element in personnel job cannot be outright rejected, though it alone does not characterize the personnel job.

It is very often reiterated by scholars that, the inherent nature of personnel job incurs many stigmata like errand running, fire fighting, shock absorbing, file clerk's job etc. The personnel executives with different degree of condemnation reacted to these stigmata characterizing the personnel job. They vehemently opposed to the errand running file clerk's nature of personnel job, as evident form 65.88 per cent and 86.67 per cent disagreeing respectively. The disagreement to the fire fighting and shock absorbing nature of personnel job have been lukewarm, as 28.23 per cent of the respondents have disagreed to the statement.

Inversely, the agreement for the challenging and respectable nature of personnel job being recorded by 85.89 per cent of the personnel executives can be considered a strong reaction to the poor portrayal of the personnel job profile.

Although the humanistic nature of personnel job is not totally accepted, yet, the understanding, analysing, predicting and modifying of human behaviour at work as a core area of personnel function is agreed by 79.61 per cent of the executives. Thus, organisational behaviour has assumed an important part in personnel job.

The personnel job of managing people at work rests on a philosophical foundations. Dichotomized as negative and positive philosophies, the manner in which people are managed at work either takes an authoritarian or democratic shape. Though personnel job is performed by line, and guided by the personnel executives as staff; yet, the ultimate philosophical base is provided by the top management. This contention has been agreed by 70.98 per cent of the respondents who relate the philosophy with the level confidence the management has in the nature and contribution of personnel job.

All the above discussions lead to infer that, the personnel job is in a transition from legalistic nature to behavioural overtones. The low profile of the personnel job is not agreed though the fire fighting and shock absorbing nature of the personnel job still retains its flavour. It has been previously found that, the career advancement opportunities followed by the scalar position of personnel executives in the organisational hierarchy, conditions of employment and decision making freedom in personnel functions are the need gap areas of personnel executives. All these relate to the inherent nature of the personnel job over which the personnel executives indicate a very low degree of satisfaction.

Opinion About the Functioning of the NIPM

The origin, growth, objectives and functions of NIPM has been highlighted in the Chapter 3. The opinion of personnel executives and academic institutes imparting training in personnel management have been sought with regard to the functioning of the NIPM in upholding the status of personnel profession. The response of the personnel executives to the question that "the role of the NIPM in bringing professional excellence is adequate", shows that 22.35 per cent have agreed, 52.16 per cent partially agreed, 23.53 per cent disagreed and 1.96 per cent have given no opinion. Mostly the respondents being members of the NIPM they are always in a better position to evaluate the functioning of the NIPM. The percentage of response of the executives tilting more towards disagreement, shows that the role of the NIPM in upholding the excellence of the profession has not been satisfactory to the respondents.

The academic institutions have given a mixed response with regard to the role of the NIPM. Three of the institutions held that they can not make any evaluation of the role of NIPM, mostly on the ground that it is the professionals who can best evaluate its working. One institution each held the working of the NIPM as satisfactory and very effective, while two institutions have held it only fair.

Summing Up

The most prevailing job title is personnel. Combined nomenclatures clubbing Labour Welfare and Industrial Relations with personnel is also largely prevailing. But, such combined nomenclatures are least preferred. Human Resources title is not only gaining currency but also greatly preferred. Despite the statutory base the Welfare designation loses its charm as it is least preferred by the responding executives. Uniform job descriptions explaining the personnel's functional responsibility is becoming difficult to have due to the variety of nomenclatures and designations, which describe either functional specializations or hierarchical positions. Yet, the evidence from the advertisements for the personnel executives reveals the split function nature of personnel job descriptions. The personnel and welfare get combined separating industrial relations. The non personnel functions looked after by the extended departments are estate, medical, security, public relations, community services, stores, telecommunications, township, transport, general administrations etc. These functions under miscellaneous categories along with the three core functions like Industrial Relation, Personnel Management and Labour Welfare are performed by personnel executives in different degrees. Industrial relations emerges as the primary functional responsibility followed by personnel administration. While miscellaneous functions are simply subsidiary in nature labour welfare becomes a combined activity. Thus, in terms of job title and functional responsibilities there is no uniform pattern.

With regard to job specification the two years degree or diploma in personnel and other related disciplines is the qualification mostly specified by the advertisements as well as possessed by the personnel executives. Even though M.B.A. degree as a specification comes next in the advertisements, such degree holders are few in terms of employment. Social Work degree with personnel as a special paper is specified sometimes for welfare officers. And such degree holders are also employed in a sizable number. Degrees in Behavioural Sciences and Human Resources Development are witnessed in advertisements but no personnel executive possesses such degrees apparently because of absence of such degrees. The 6 months diploma courses are some what popular where the organisations seek only work experiences and prefer to depute such non-qualified executives for short duration courses. This practice needs to be viewed with concern as the personnel executives believe that such courses are not adequate to tackle the complexities of the personnel job. Similar opinion is also held about general management courses and pure social work courses.

The academic institutions, which are supposed to cater to the specifications of organisations in terms of turning out qualified personnel executives, lack uniformity in their course content and teaching methods. The institutes fully devoted to personnel management and other related courses give more intensive training in personnel management, organisational behaviour, industrial relations, labour welfare, labour legislation etc., the business management institute and social work schools. Such courses are considered more useful by the practising personnel executives in their day-to-day work. Field work as a practical training though offered by the institutes yet as a learning method its utility is considered low by the personnel executives. Training in computers is not offered excepting by few business management institutes. The responding executives also do not claim to have received such training. However, the utility of computers in personnel profession is greatly appreciated.

Lecture, seminars, conferences and case analysis are the commonly used methods by the institutes which are considered beneficial by the personnel executives. Participative learning techniques like games, role playing and advanced devices like audio visual technology and computers are sparsely used, though considered quite beneficial for augmenting the professional qualifications.

Alongwith the deficiencies in the course curricula and teachings methods, the role played by the personnel executives, academic institutions and industrial organisations in enriching the discipline base of personnel profession is quite discouraging. Participation in seminars, conferences by the personnel executives are only to keep abreast of the latest developments. Their contribution to the professional literature is very less. Similarly the academic institutions barring intermittent interactions with industrial organisations for the purposes of the academic research, hardly establish a constant contact with the practices. Action research initiated by the organisations is few and far between. So also is the case with personnel research as a personnel function. Consultancy in personnel area is largely confined to either labour law practitioners or few business management institutions. Placement programmes are a contact area between the academic institutions and industrial organisations but it does not help in enriching the personnel discipline. Thus, the personnel profession is not having a sound discipline base.

In course of their day-to-day activities the personnel executives interact with top management, line executives and trade unions. Reflecting on the relations with them the personnel executives have exhibited a greater satisfaction level. On the other hand their satisfaction level is relatively low with regard to their job content, conditions and job offers. Lack of promotional avenues is identified as the main need gap area. Yet, the executives believe that competence on the job, professional qualifications and previous experience are move decisive in ensuring promotion than personnel contacts, recommendations and such other unethical practices. Industrial relations being the primary function of personnel department its fire fighting and shock absorbing role often invites the wrath of the union. Logically the unions contended that the personnel departments are used by the management to harass workers and are pseudo neutral. However, the executives viewed that their industrial relations function is misunderstood for its 'watch dog' and 'police role'. Denouncing there redundant statutory status and functions of welfare officers the executives strongly favour the practice of management's free handling organising the welfare function. The personnel executives equivocally wished to rely more on their advisory and assisting role than on the decision making forte. They believed that should advice and timely assistance can have the same effect of a control on the line. Reflecting on the changing nature of the job the executives opined that it is in a transition from legalistic to behavioristic nature. The low profile of the personnel job is strongly refuted. The role of NIPM in uplifting the personnel profession is respondent with a lukewarm appreciation.

ANNEXURE-I

Name of the Educational Institutes devoted to the Training in Personnel Management.

1. Department of Industrial Relations and Personnel Management, Andhra University, Visakhapatnam.
2. Department of Personnel Management and Labour Welfare, Utkal University, Bhubaneswar.

3. Department of Personnel Management, Xavier Institute of Social Science, Ranchi.
4. Department of Labour Welfare, Gujarat University, Ahmedabad.
5. Department of Personnel Management and Labour Welfare, Kurukshetra University, Haryana.
6. Department of Labour and Social Welfare, Patna University, Patna.
7. Department of Industrial Relations, Xavier Labour Relations Institute, Jameshedpur.
8. Department of Personnel Management and Industrial Relations, Tata Institute of Social Sciences, Bombay.
9. Department of Social Work, University of Delhi, Delhi.
10. Department of Social Work, Jamia Millia Islamia, Delhi.
11. Department of Social Work, Visva Bharti, Shantiniketan.
12. Department of Social Work (Labour Welfare), Indian Institute of Social Welfare and Business Management, Calcutta.
13. Department of Social Work, Udaipur School of Social Work, Udaipur.
14. Department of Social Work, Kashividyapith, Varanasi.
15. Madras School of Social Work Madras.
16. Department of Social Work, Sri Padmavati Mahila Viswavidyalayam, Tirupati.
17. Department of Social Work, University of Lucknow, Lucknow.
18. Department of Social Work, Maharaja Sayaji Rao University of Baroda, Baroda.
19. Department of Social Work, Bangalore University, Bangalore.
20. Department of Social Work, Karantaka University, Dharwar.
21. J.P. Institute of Social and Industrial Studies, Ranchi.
22. Bharathidasan Institute of Management, Tiruchirapalli.
23. Department of Social Work, Andhra University, Visakhapatnam.

24. Department of Labour and Social Welfare, Bhagalpur University, Bhagalpur.
25. Department of Labour and Social Welfare, Magadha University, Bodh Gaya, Bihar.
26. Department of Personnel Management and Industrial Relations, Indian Institute of Management, Calcutta.
27. Department of Management Studies, Indian Institute of Management, Ahmedabad.
28. Department of Management Studies, Indian Institute of Management, Lucknow.
29. Department of Management Studies, Indian Institute of Management, Bangalore.
30. Department of Management Studies, Cochin University, Cochin.
31. Institute of Management, Bharatiya Vidya Bhawan, Baroda.

ANNEXURE-II

Name of the Responding Educational Institutes

1. Madras School of Social Work, Madras.

*2. Sri Padamavati Mahila Viswavidyalayam, Tirupati.

3. Department of Social Work, Kurukshetra University.
4. Department of Labour Welfare, Gujarat University, Gujarat.
5. Department of Social Work, Delhi University.
6. Department of Industrial Relations and Personnel Management, Andhra University.
7. Department of Labour Welfare, Utkal University.
8. Indian Institute of Management, Ahmedabad.

---

* This institute reported that it does not provide specialisation in Personnel Management. So it has been excluded.

9. Indian Institute of Management, Lucknow.
10. Indian Institute of Management, Bangalore.
11. Department of Management Studies, Cochin University.

List of Institutes whose syllabi was received through the Department of I.R.P.M., Berhampur University.

1. Department of Economics, Mysore University.
2. Department of Commerce, Mysore University.
3. Xavier Institute of Social Services, Ranchi.
4. Department of Social Work, Jamia Millia Islamia, Delhi.
5. Indian Institute of Social Welfare and Business Management, Calcutta.

*6. Annamalai University.

7. Department of Social Work, Viswabharati.

*8. National Institute of Personnel Management.

---

* The University and Institute provide diploma in personnel management through correspondence course.

ANNEXURE-III

List of Industrial Organisations contacted for the purpose of Study

1. Asian Paint Pack Limited, Bangalore.
2. Bajaj Electricals Limited, Bombay.
3. Bata India Limited, Batanagar.
4. Bombay Port Trust, Bombay.
5. Damodar Valley Corporation, Calcutta.
6. East India Pharmaceutical Works Limited, Calcutta.
7. Gas Authority of India Limited, New Delhi.
8. H.M.T (Machine Tools Division), Bangalore.

9. Hindustan Aeronautics Limited, Bangalore.
10. Hindustan paper Corporation Limited, Calcutta.
11. Indian Airlines, New Delhi.
12. Bharat Heavy Electricals Limited, New Delhi.
13. Krishak Bharati Cooperative Limited, New Delhi.
14. Coal India limited, Calcutta.
15. Indian Oil Corporation Limited, New Delhi.
16. Industrial Development Corporation of Orissa Limited, Bhubaneswar.
17. Integral Coach Factory, Madras.
18. Kerala Chemicals and Proteins Limited, Cochin.
19. Mahindra and Mahindra Limited, Bombay.
20. National Thermal Power Corporation Limited, New Delhi.
21. Neyveli Lignite Corporation Limited, Neyveli.
22. Oil and Natural Gas Commission, Dehradun.
23. Reliance Industries Limited, Ahmedabad.
24. Scooters India Limited, Lucknow.
25. Steel Authority of India, New Delhi.
26. Tata Iron and Steel Company, Jameshedpur.
27. Union Carbide India Limited, Calcutta.
28. United Bank of India, Calcutta.
29. Usha Martin Black, Bangalore.
30. Visakhapatnam Port Trust, Visakhapatnam.
31. Voltas Limited, Bombay.
32. Indian Rare Earths limited, Bombay.
33. Bajaj Auto Limited, Poona.

34. Oil India Limited, Allahabad.
35. Hindustan Prefeb Limited, New Delhi.
36. International Airport Authority of India Limited, New Delhi.
37. Indian Oxygen Limited, Calcutta.
38. Uptron India Limited, Lucknow.
39. Vijaya Bank, Bangalore.
40. South India Viscous Limited, Coimbatore.
41. Glaxo Laboratories India Limited, Bombay.
42. Gaman India Limited, Bombay.
43. Indian Metals and Ferro Alloys Limited, Bhubaneswar.
44. Ideal Jawa India Private Limited, Mysore.
45. Toshiba Anand Batteries Limited, Cochin.
46. Hindustan Level Limited, Bombay.
47. Sylvania & Laxman Limited, New Delhi.
48. Kores India Limited, Bombay.
49. Escorts Limited, New Delhi.

ANNEXURE-IV

List of the Trade Union Organisations contacted for the purpose of the study.

*1. President, AITUC, New Delhi.

2. Secretary, AITUC, Orissa Branch, Cuttack.

*3. President, INTUC, Orissa Branch, Bhubaneswar.

4. President, HMS., Rourkela.

*5. General Secretary, CITU, Bhubaneswar.

*6. President, BMS, Cuttack.

7. President, BMS, Orissa Branch, Rourkela.
8. Secretary, NFITU, Bhubaneswar.
9. President, INTUC, New Delhi.
10. Secretary, INTUC, New Delhi.
11. President, Tata Workers' Union, Jamshedpur.
12. General Secretary, INTUC, New Delhi.
13. Secretary, AITUC, New Delhi.
14. President, All India central Govt, Employees' Union, New Delhi.

---

* Indicate the name of the Trade Union Organisations responded.

REFERENCES

1. This list does not claim itself to be final as there is a mushroom growth in management institutes in recent years. However, care has been taken to cover all premier institutes of the country.
2. McFarland considers labour relations and personnel as the two core functions basing on which he explains these three categories. However, keeping in view the statutory position of welfare in India, the present division considers three core areas namely, Industrial Relations, Personnel Management and Labour Welfare. McFarland, *Personnel*, p.82.

5

Evaluating the Professional Status of Personnel and Predicting its Future in India

Introduction

In consonance with the research objectives, the previous three chapters have been devoted to the past and present of personnel profession in India. Now, picking up the threads from such a temporal presentation of facts and opinions, this chapter sets forth to serve two important purposes namely; evaluating the professional status of personnel and predicting its future which are presented in two parts. Despite the exclusive treatment they receive in the discussions, these purposes are mutually complementary and are meant to complete the temporal cycle. With its integrative approach, this chapter addresses to the task of carefully analysing the personnel occupation as it moves towards professionalisation so as to determine its locus standi on the professional continuum and to predict the future course it will take. Tho framework of analysis, as pointed out in Chapter 1, would cut across the three identified dimensions such as professional features; clientele served; the elitist status of personnel professionals. The factors that influence the professionalisation of personnel occupation namely, industrialization process, emergence of an industrial work-force, welfarism, emergence of trade unionism and industrial relations functions and other developments at different periods of time in India (as discussed in Chapter 2, 3 and 4) provide the base for the analysis and prediction. Thus, this chapter embodies the findings and conclusions of the study.

PART – I

EVALUATING THE CURRENT STATUS OF PERSONNEL PROFESSION

Theoretical Framework

The assumption that is clearly spell out at the outset of the study is that, "the Personnel occupation by its very history has proved that it has attempted to professionalise itself since its very inception". So, on the professionalisation continuum personnel occupation has already made a move. The experiences of U.S.A. and U.K. in this regard, whose impact on India needs no reiteration, lends support to this assumption. In terms of early attempts at forming professional bodies, at turning out professional literature, at initiating training programmes, at developing standards of ethics; the manner in which the personnel occupation preceded general management prompts one to accept this assumption virtually as a contention. So, this study does not enter into the debate as to whether personnel occupation is a profession or not. Rather it firmly upholds that, personnel occupation is in the process of professionalisation, though there is a difference in the degree. This justifies the bringing in of the professional continuum concept and the temporal analysis the study wished to have with regard to the past, present and future of personnel profession in India.

The conceptual contours of the study after identifying the feature that an occupation need to possess in order to qualify as a profession, highlighted the semantic expressions of the terms professionalisation and professionalism. The occupation gets professionalised while the incumbents achieve professionalism. Hence, the possibilities of achieving higher degree of professionalism within a profession is always there although some degree of professionalisation is *sine qua non* for achieving professionalism. Further, the possibilities of occupations simulating professional features and partly fulfilling the feature while in a transit have been identified as issues in evaluating any occupation as a profession.

Two more dimensions which have been identified as parameters to measure the professional status of an occupation are clientele served and elitist status ascribed. Bringing in the concepts of 'cosmopolitan' and 'local' professions, the size and structure of clientele has been treated as a yardstick to measure the degree of professionalisation achieved. Further, by bringing the concept of 'agreed clientele' and 'clientele of one's choice', the notion of faith in the professional's competence and intentions have been highlighted as much as the degree of autonomy the professional enjoys in pursuing his profession. Lastly, the elitist status of professionals as an ascribed status associated with socially approved role behaviour has been taken as an identifying factor in understanding the degree of professionalisation on occupation has achieved.

Features of Personnel Profession in India

Emergence of Personnel Function and Function-aries in India

The personnel function in India like that of U.K. and U.S.A. has emerged after industrial development. The mid-nineteenth century witnessed the beginning of industrialization under the aegis of British entrepreneurs who developed mining, plantation and some manufacturing industries like textile, jute and tanneries, besides laying a railway network as an import infrastructure. Yet the initial pace of industrialization was slow partly due to the British policy of *Lessaize Faire* and partly due to non-availability of requisite skill, capital and entrepreneurship among the Indians. It was only after 1875 that the factory system began to progress and by the first decade of 20th Century Indian entrepreneurs like Tatas and Birlas and others provided leadership to industrialization. While the Inter-War period witnessed a boom in the industrialization, the second World War gave a fillip to it. From a paltry 656 factories in 1892, it rose upto 14,576 by the year 1947 thereby registering a 22.2 fold increase, while improving the employment rate by 7.17 fold (i.e., 316816 in 1892 and 2274689 in 1947).

Along the lines of such growth in industrialization and concomitant rise in the employment of industrial work-force; problems of migration mounted up with associated tendency of village nexus. So, in the initial stages, the industrial workers had no commitment to the industrial ways of life. The problems of absenteeism and labour turnover during this period were so rampant that a steady supply of labour was the dire need of the factories. The jobbers as local intermediaries became handy for the British employers for they procured, supervised and extracted work from the workers. Their exercise of power became so very crude that the Royal Commission on Labour (RCL) took great exception to this system and suggested appointment of Labour Officers to look after hiring of employees. An important personnel function like procurement and a functionary in 'labour officer' designation thus emerged.

The emergence of trade unionism in late 19th Century with a slow but steady pace and statutory recognition it received in 1926 after many trials and tribulations, marked the beginning of industrial relations as a crucial function in personnel management. However, the way employers responded to this function of dealing with trade unions was very discouraging because by appointing police and military personnel, the idea probably was to curb trade unionism. Yet, the trade unions emerged with their own efforts in a unconducive environment contributed by virtual apathy of the British Government in India. The need for collective bargaining further strengthened the industrial relations function.

Welfarism as a paternalistic concern was advocated by some employers and were undertaken by social philanthropic agencies. The inter-war period developments, specially the formation of ILO, and the recommendations of RCL succeeded in the enactment of few factory and social security legislations, which had great impact on the emergence of welfare function in India. The recognition given to welfare as an efficiency boosting measure during and after the First World War further strengthened the welfare component of the personnel function.

All these developments traced above find their roots in labour legislations. Beginning with the Apprentices Act, 1850; the passing of different legislations like the Factories Acts of 1911, 1922, 1934; Social Security Laws like Workmen's Compensation Act, 1923; Trade Unions Act, 1926; the Trade Disputes Act, 1929 and 1934; and Payment of Wages Act, 1936; paved the path for the welfare and industrial relations functions in industrial set up. The need for complying with the provisions of these legislations was greatly felt and labour officers and/or labour lawyers were entrusted with this task by early 1930s. There functions were further expanded with the enactment of the Industrial Employment (Standing Orders) Act, 1946.

This is how the three core functions of personnel management namely, employment and other labour administration functions, industrial relations and welfare functions emerged in India. However, the then welfare workers, or the police and military personnel or the labour officers might get the recognition as precursors of the present day personnel executives, but they were never professionals. At this point it is pertinent to highlight the fact that personnel designation was not a post-independent import from the U.S.A. as commonly held; rather it was prevailing in the Indian railways to denote a department although. But labour officer designation was the popular nomenclature of these who performed the personnel function.

The contention that, the labour officers in the pre-independent India were hardly professionals can be substantiated by the lack of any specific qualifications prescribed for them by the RCL. Integrity, personality, energy, the gift of understanding individuals, the linguistic facility which are more personality traits than specialised qualifications were expected from a labour officer by the RCL. Neither was there any prescribed qualification nor any scope for acquiring training. So, hardly there was any discipline base for this function. The attempts of Sir Dorabji Tata Graduate School of Social Work, Bombay (1936) (later renamed as Tata Institute of Social Sciences) was to give a social work orientation borrowed from U.S.A. mostly to augment the philanthropic activities of voluntary agencies. Excepting influencing welfare component of personnel function, social work orientation was of little help in providing a discipline base. The in-service training programmes organised by the Indian Jute Mills Association under the banner of Indian Institute of Social Welfare and Business Management at Calcutta (1942) mostly provided workable knowledge about labour legislations. Thus, hardly was there any discipline base or training facility in personnel management prior to 1947.

The prevalence of patrimonial managers in private family run organisations and of political/bureaucratic managers in government agencies in the pre-independent India stifled professionalism in general management. In this context the very fact that personnel being a part of general management was not adequately professionalised appears to be logical.

Nevertheless, the emergence of distinct function and functionaries in personnel, the early attempts to devise course structure for imparting training to the functionaries and other developments in pre-independent India are small yet sure steps towards professionalisation.

Consolidation of Personnel Function and Functionaries (1947 onwards)

The post-independent India experimented with the planning process for improving its economy. Following this there has been a spurt in industrial activity and the industrial work-force registered an almost 2.5 times increase. Similar trend could be witnessed in the number of working factories and employment rate in those factories. The liberalization of technology import policies, and improvements in indigenous technology demanded skilled workers. By sponsoring training institutes and by augmenting the process of education this demand has been partly fulfilled. However, in view of the vast manpower size and potential industrial edifice the extent of human resources development has been at best marginal.

Compounding the problem is the low commitment of the workers to the industrial way of life. The rural-urban exodus as a result of industrialization might have decreased. But, the lopsided distribution of industrialization in the country and the resultant economic disparity contribute to migration of job-seekers from underdeveloped areas to developed areas. While the village nexus character might have decreased in its effect; yet, the alarming proportions the problem of absenteeism is taking in organisations can be indicative of lack of commitment on the part of the industrial workers. Such a work-force, which on account of skill development nourish high aspirations and right consciousness and simultaneously exhibit low duty consciousness and commitment, obviously pose an important challenge to the personnel profession whose main object is to utilize the 'human resources'.

Growth in trade unionism is noteworthy in quantitative terms. There has been a 13.34 fold increase in the number of trade unions in 1985 over 1947-48. The total union membership has, however, registered only 4.62 fold increase. This indicates that the growth in membership is quite disproportionate to the growth in the number of unions. Only 30 per cent of the workers in the organised sector are unionized. Besides the poor membership following, the trade unions in India suffer from many shortcomings. Politicized since inception, the unionism is dominated by outside leaders. Multiplicity and mushroom growth of unions contributed by the statutory provisions and multiple political parties (each one of whom foster a trade union) result into active inter and intra union rivalries. A fragmented trade union movement coupled with declining membership following make the unions organizationally and financially weak. The feeling of the members that the trade unions are meant to work for them and not with them is contributing in making the leaders strategically militant in order to impress upon the members that the union is active. Militancy devoid of bargaining strength in terms of involvement of the workers often result in unions ending with dead loss for the workers.

Collective bargaining in this context of trade unionism is neither institutionalized nor does in play the decisive role in tackling with industrial conflict. The enactment of the Industrial Disputes Act, 1947; followed by the Government policy favouring adjudication over collective bargaining as the ultimate method of solving industrial disputes; once for all stifled the chances of collective bargaining institution in India. The spate of industrial unrest experienced in the early periods of post-independent India could be a reason for the Government intervention as opposed to free collective bargaining. This situation, of course, is argued by some as favourable to healthy collective bargaining as a voluntary measure providing scope for the true bipartite negotiation. The militancy of trade unions coupled with weak bargaining strength of the workers has resulted in making the industrial relations situation in the country somewhat disturbed. This is evident from the frequency rate and severity rate of industrial disputes which have registered 1.5 folds and 8.5 folds increase respectively during the years 1951-86.

Taking into account the cause-wise distribution of the disputes, the economic issues like wages, bonus and incentives are prominent. From among the non-economic causes, conditions of work and employment account for one third of the disputes. Indiscipline and violence emerged as separate cause since 1968. For personnel professionals in India to-day, the industrial relations function is posing many challenges.

A number of legislations were enactment in free India either to protect the labour standards and to improve the working conditions, or to regulate employer-employee relations; or to provide social security provisions, whose compliance has become a core area of personnel function.

In terms of generating a new functionary in personnel, the contributions of Factories Act, 1948 followed by the Plantation Act and Mines Act are noteworthy for the provision of 'Welfare Officer'. The conditions of service and duties of the Welfare officer, being regulated by Law and rules made thereof, have created peculiar problems in the functioning of the officers which has far reaching consequences for the personnel profession. The head of the department status, neutral position, the protection that the Welfare Officer is assigned under the law have all been proved by practice as ostentatious. Treated as a legal imposition by the management, this office is accommodated in the organisation as a compliance but not as a necessity. In practice welfare offer's occupational status is relegated to personnel. The institution of welfare officer with its dubious role definition has earned some stigma like 'third force', 'linking pin', 'buffer zone', 'fire fighter', 'non-allied profeşsional' for the personnel profession.

The Inherent Nature of Personnel Job

The job title and the designation of the department dealing with human resources are quite varied. Besides the term 'personnel' such other designations namely 'Labour Welfare', 'industrial relations' are used as job titles and designations. The size and structure of the organization and the management culture associated with the sectoral differences are the causes attributed for different nomenclatures. However, it is the personnel designation which dominates as evident from the advertisements as well as the designations possessed and preferred by the sample personnel executives. There is a considerable prevalence of combined designations in which personnel becomes the main title with industrial relations and administrative appended to it. This is of course lowly preferred by the executives. Of late the Human Resources Management title is gaining currency which appears to be catching popularity as the personnel executives greatly prefer it.

There is a consensus about the three core functional areas of personnel management despite the lack of uniformity in the title. These are Personnel Administration, Industrial Relations and Labour Welfare. The organisation of these three responsibilities had no uniform pattern. There are integrated, split function and extended departments with either production or welfare orientation. The analysis of job description from the advertisements indicate that the split-function nature of organising the personnel function is the most popular with around 70 per cent accounting for it. The three core areas are mostly bifurcated in the split-function nature of the organization. In this process personnel is mostly combined with labour welfare separating industrial relations function. Over and above the core functions, the many extraneous functions like estate, transport, medical, security, township, public relations, etc. characterize the job description thereby making such departments extended in nature. Around 14 per cent of the advertisements account for such job description. Around 16 per cent of the advertisement account for integrated nature of organising the personnel function.

Industrial relations emerge as the main function actually performed by the personnel executives dominating over all others. It is followed by personnel and labour welfare in that order. The miscellaneous functions which are of extended nature dominate as subsidiary function. The dominance of industrial relations in the functional domain of personnel executives, despite the prominence of personnel nomenclature as the job title, when is viewed in the light of union's opinion about the personnel department and personnel executive's opinion about the union, makes important revelations.

In the industrial relations activities, the main role of the personnel executives is to deal with unions. Constant interaction between them is imperative. In this process both size up each other and develop strategies. The personnel executives on account of their union handling role do face typical problems and criticisms. The opinions tendered by the unions and personnel executives indicate the precarious nature of the personnel job. The executives largely agreed that the union's attitude towards the personnel department is not encouraging. The unions equivocally became critical of the personnel department. The unions neutrality stance of the personnel department, its dubious role of prohibiting unfair labour practices, its ability to harass the workers are the opinions which indicate union's lack of faith in the personnel job. However, by agreeing to the contention that the personnel department is used as a protective shield by the line and chief executives, the union appears to be sympathetic towards the fire fighting nature of the personnel job. It is pertinent to observe here that, miliancy of the union leaders as a substitute behaviour to the lack of their organisational strength causes lots of stress and strain on the personnel job who bear the direct brunt of the union onslaught and this sometimes becomes even physically risky. So long as the relations with the unions are maintained and an ostensible peace reigns in the organisation, the personnel department hardly gets recognised as successful. But, with small tremors of unrest, the department gets blamed. This majority opinion of the executives indicate the state of self pity in which they find themselves. The demands of the personnel job as is to have strategic relations with the unions, prompt line and other executives to disbelieve the personnel job as potential trouble shoots. Thus, the industrial relations component of the personnel job makes the profession quite challenging, stressful and risky.

The personnel administration component of the personnel job, involving access to classified information pertaining to employees and with some quantity of reward power enjoined upon the job, subjects it to criticism by fellow executives of other departments, workers and unions. Although the establishment nature of the personnel role provides some amount of maneuverability to the personnel department; yet, it equally incurs the wrath and displeasure of the employees. The unions find opportunity to create an issue out of this role. Thus, the personnel job largely becomes a critical one.

The welfare component of the personnel job nevertheless brings disrepute to the personnel profession, on account of earning such stigmata as 'errand running', 'cafeteria managing', 'file clerk', etc. The rendundant statutory provisions coupled with the long standing frustrated experience with this officer subscribe to this finding. Thus, the three core functional areas in no way enhance the professional status of personnel.

The overtly legalistic nature of the personnel job in terms of complying with the provisions of different labour legislations, and specially in the nature of handling industrial relations has been largely agreed by the executives. However, their opinion demonstrates a reservation for the humanistic overtones of the personnel job. The behavioural dynamics involved in the managing of human resources at work are considered important ingredients of the personnel job. Thus, the personnel job is undergoing changes.

One of the important dynamics emanating from the inherent nature of personnel job is its staff nature. The staff role of personnel centres round advice and service as specialists rather than on the decision making forte. The personnel executives strongly favour this contention. Strategies for making the staff service imperative for the line lie with the persuasiveness, expertise and genuineness of the advice rendered by the personnel is a contention largely agreed by the personnel executives. By expressing satisfaction over their relations with the line and chief executives, the personnel executives set at rest the apprehension about the conflict proneness of line-staff relations. However, the personnel executives by expressing low satisfaction over the decision-making freedom they really enjoy indicate that there are few areas in personnel function which still permit decision making role.

The personnel executives express low satisfaction over the conditions of their employment, scalar position of their department in the organisation and career advancement opportunities. The dissatisfaction of the executives with regard to the conditions of the employment and scalar position of the department can be attributed to the low treatment meted out to them in the organisations. The personnel department is very often placed at a lower echelon to the works and other line departments as well as to some staff departments like Finance. Thereby the salary and other perquisites of personnel staff get reduced in comparison to other departmental heads. Further, the instances of personnel executives rising to the position of chief executive officers are so few and far between that they indicate the dead and nature of the personnel profession.

It is appropriate to note the trends of some erstwhile personnel functions like training and development breaking away to be recognised as distinct function and some functions like recruitment and adjudication being assigned to outside consultants and/or legal practitioners. Similarly, some new functions arising out of introduction of behaviouralism and computers get added to the personnel function. In this way, the inherent nature of the personnel job is under a constant flux. All these findings converge upon to the inference that, the personnel profession is in a constant search for a distinct identity. It is not known by a common nomenclature. Nor there are defined functional boundaries of this profession. It serves the organizations only. Even in this respect the professionals find the job quite stressful and risky. Due to the functional flux there is a scope for role ambiguity.

Job Specification and Training Base of the Personnel Profession

The three core functional activities of the personnel profession had distinctly emerged prior to independence. The functionaries were mostly either labour officers, a designation advanced by RCL or administrative officers drawn mostly from military and police personnel ostensibly to ward off law and order situation created by the unions. However, in either of the cases there was no prescription of specialised qualifications. The traces of welfarism found in the then personnel action with social work overtones prompted the Tata group of industries to start a social work school in the year 1936. Just prior to independence the Bengal Jute Mills Association found the need for updating the knowledge of officers in the growing labour legislations. This was responsible for the opening of an institute at Calcutta which used to provide short duration diploma courses to in-service officers. Thus, there was neither a definite job specification of personnel profession nor strong training base prior to independence.

The Central Model Rules for welfare officers in the year 1951 (following the enactment of Factories Act, 1948) by incorporating the duties, qualifications and conditions of employment of Welfare Officers provided a definite job specification. With its welfare dominance the training base of such officers more or less retained social work orientation. As a result many social work institutes with labour welfare as a field of specialisation emerged soon after independence. Being influenced by the labour school concept of U.S.A. specially of Cornell University, Labour & Social Welfare Departments were started in India. These two developments occurred contemporaneously. With the enactment of Industrial Disputes Act, the industrial relations function with its legalistic overtones demanded training in industrial relations. The implementation and enforcement of various labour legislations necessitated training in labour legislation. With greater exposure to the exposure to the American personnel management theory, the erstwhile procuring and other maintenance functions along with industrial relations, labour welfare and labour legislation were brought under and a common label called 'personnel'. A transformation from labour and social welfare to industrial relations and then to personnel management occurred on an evolutionary basis. Such educational institutes include in their course structure subjects like general management, personnel management, industrial relations, labour welfare administration, labour legislation, collective bargaining, trade unions, field work and other areas.

The management education under the aegis of IIMs since 1962 opened a new chapter in turning out professional managers. These and other management institutes treated personnel as one of the branches alongwith marketing, production, finance etc. However, the coverage of these institutes with regard to personnel management and other related areas was much less than the institutes devoted to pure personnel management training. In this way the training base of personnel profession got built up without any uniform pattern.

The main qualification as prescribed in the advertisements for entry into personnel profession is degree or diploma in personnel management and other related areas. MBA degree holders are also preferred but not to the extent of personnel degree holders. Degree in Law is an additional qualification and social work degree is not that popular. The contention of Union Carbide that training in general management is not adequate to tackle the complex personnel problems further substantiates the need for specialised training in personnel. More than one third of the responding personnel executives, by possessing two year degree in personnel management and around 80 per cent of them finding such degree fully adequate for the profession, reiterate the inference drawn above.

However, the prevalence of eleven varieties of prescribed qualification (Table 4.11), the nine varieties of degree possessed by the practising professionals (Table 4.12) indicate that, there is no uniformity in the job specification of personnel. Yet, the two year degree in personnel is the most prominent specialisation. Relating this finding with the personnel designation dominating over others and with the industrial relations and personnel as primary functions, it can be rightly concluded that personnel management is emerging as a distinct field of specialisation.

The subjects offered, teaching methods adopted by the academic Institutes alongwith the training exposure of the personnel executives indicate a wide variety. There is no uniform course content within each group of academic institutes and also between the institutes under each category. The social work schools and business management schools offer personnel subjects as compulsory and/or electives. Whereas the pure personnel management institutes provide a more extensive and intensive training programme incorporating various subjects including field work. The personnel executives have in different degree received training in various subjects of personnel management (Table 4.17). And they find personnel management, industrial relations and labour legislations highly useful in their day-to-day activities followed by industrial psychology, organisational behaviour and labour welfare administration. Training in computers is least available, sparsely possessed though largely considered as essential. Despite the lack of uniformity in the course structure, there is a consistency in the teaching methods adopted by the academic institutions. Lecture method being the most used one, the participant teaching methods are supplemental in nature. However, the personnel executives strongly favour the case analysis and such other participative techniques as more beneficial than the lecture method. In this respect the business management institutes with their monopoly on consultation services find themselves in a better place to collect and disseminate live cases in comparison to the pure personnel management institutes. Thus, in respect of job specification and training base there is a wide variety of practices available in India.

Discipline Base of Personnel Profession

Personnel as a discipline owed its origin to social work. With the expansion of the personnel function, the discipline base also widened and influenced by various social sciences got enriched. The discipline under the impact of the western management literature emerged as a management science. Further enrichment of the discipline came through the influence of the behavioural sciences.

In this process of evolution from social work to management/ behaviroual science, the personnel discipline in India initially relied heavily upon the western theories. But, in due course attempts have been made by a host of scholars from India and abroad to study the typical local conditions through empiricism and *in situ* research. However, these attempts appear to be more devoted to the validation of western theories in the Indian context than for the purpose of culture specific theorizing. The text book boom only turns out to be compilation of western theories supported by Indian cases. Thus, the volume of personnel discipline although has increased in leaps and bounds; yet, its quality leaves with ground for improvement.

Theory is advanced by practiced and practice is disciplined by theory equally holds good for personnel profession. The academic institutes as the enricher of theory and personnel executives as vanguards of practice cannot compartmentalize their roles. Both have to constantly interact in the organizational setting. Then only the discipline base of the personnel professional can be enriched. The interaction at the training stage through field work placements is extremely limited. The students as part fulfilment of their courses are placement in organizations to collect some information and ostensibly acquire practical training. The output of such placement is embodied in the form of project reports/dissertations containing half baked informations. The purpose of field work placements never get realise due to the half hearted initiation and response of the academic institutes and industrial organizations respectively. Depending on the proximity of the organization to the academic institutes, concurrent field work would be more advantageous than block field work. The prevalence of concurrent field work is very limited. The response made by the personnel executives indicating that their field work training has not been useful in their day-to-day activities, further substantiates the inadequacies of field work in abridging the gap between theory and practice.

Personnel research either initiated by organizations as a part of personnel function or by the academic institutions for the purpose of awarding degrees is a potential contact area between organizations and academic institutes. Personnel research hardly receives the status of a distinct personnel function in Indian organizations. Action research fully supported by organizations and involved by academic institutes is totally absent. The personnel executives admit that they seldom contribute to journals which is indicative of their lack of interest in professional literature. Attendance in seminars and conferences is relatively better, which helps them to keep abreast of the recent theories besides providing a scope for outing at the organizations' cost. The academic institutes engaged in personnel research do have the primary purpose of acquiring degrees. The research findings based on the facts and figures collected from the organizations are not communicated to them, thereby not having any relevance for the improvement of organizations. As a result, the personnel discipline does not grow in any way in India.

Consultancy as a method of applying organizational theory for the solution of organizational problems is a forum for enriching the personnel discipline. Many private firms in the forms of management consultants, legal practitioners and procuring consultants are emerging. It is only the business management institutes which mostly indulge in consultancy. While organizational problems apparently get solved and the private consultants and business management institutes get handsomely paid; the feed back to theory from these consultancy experiences is virtually lacking. In the training stage, the case studies developed from consultancy do really help. But, in enriching the discipline the degree of feedback required from the consultancy is lacking. Thus, in all respects the personnel discipline is unable to grow taking into account the culture specific peculiar features of India. Western theories are imitated. Innovation is virtually lacking. The blame need to be equally apportioned by the academicians who are buried in their books and by the practitioners and organization who are too engrossed in practice.

Role of the Professional Body

The personnel executives organised themselves as a body of professionals earlier to the management professional body. The IIPM formed in 1948 and NILM in 1950 worked separately till 1980. The merger of these two organizations resulted in the formation of NIPM as the sole professional body of the personnel executives. The NIPM addresses itself to the realisation of 29 objectives. Besides setting out self-regulatory objectives, the NIPM strives to improve the discipline base, training base of the personnel profession. While enhancing the occupational status is an important objective, NIPM envisages to act as a pressure group on the Government, local bodies and other forums for the improvement in the labour legislations and in the over all working of the various machineries meant for maintaining employee-employer relationship. In order to realise these objectives, the NIPM conducts seminars, sponsors study teams, collects and disseminates employment information. It also publishes monographs and research papers prepared by the members and brings out a quarterly journal titled '*Personnel To-day*'. The various branch offices bring out news letters/bulletins. The association gives 'Most Distinguished Service Medal' for felicitating a member for his/her outstanding contribution to the profession. It has also instituted medals to the successful candidates who get top rank from the institutes awarding degrees or diplomas in the Personnel Management and Industrial Relations.

Comparing the professional body of the personnel executives with that of the establishment professions notably law and medicine some important inferences can be drawn. The NIPM as a voluntary body is registered under the Societies Registration Act, 1860, whereas its counterparts in that of Law and Medicine have a statutory base. The Bar Council of India, a professional body of advocates is constituted as per the provisions (section 4) of the Advocates Act, 1961. Similarly the Indian Medical Council as a professional body of medical practitioners is constituted under the provisions of the Indian Medical Council Act, 1956. The Acts inter alia make provisions for accreditation and certification of the professionals seeking entry into the respective professions. The conduct and etiquette of the legal practitioners and the code of ethics of the medical practitioners are legally set out whose branch may result into the decertification of the professionals. But, in personnel profession, neither there is any accreditation programme nor its code of ethics has legal compulsions. Personnel, in this regard, has not reached its full stature as profession is a finding that can be made in this comparative analysis.

The personnel executives as members of the NIPM when evaluate the performance of NIPM in bringing out professional excellence negatively, the opinion need to be viewed with concern. The academic institutes by observing they are not in a position to evaluate the effectiveness of NIPM suggest that as a forum the NIPM has failed to bring together the practitioners and academicians. Thus the overall performance of NIPM is not encouraging.

Evaluating the Personnel Profession by its Features

The personnel occupation in India has incorporated all the basic features of a profession. This inference can be conclusively drawn from the preceding discussions. With a relatively long history starting from the turn of this century and with a slow pace of development prior to independence; the personnel profession experienced an accelerated growth after the independence. Despite all these, its features have not matured.

As evident from the findings, the body of knowledge in personnel has quantitatively increased but qualitatively remained mostly a copy book of Western theories. Culture specific theorisation in personnel literature is an important need gap area in the maturation of the discipline base. Similar trend can be observed in the training base which is characterised by lack of uniformity in course curricula, in teaching methods and infrastructure. All these contribute to a mushroom yet qualitatively poor growth of institutes imparting training in personnel. The virtual lack of clinical support in the training base neither enriches the discipline nor provides a strong practical foundation. Thus, it imbibes the flaws of a pseudoscience and intuitions of an art.

The professional body of the personnel in India is a registered body only. Like the legal or medical profession getting bound by Acts enacted by the Government, the personnel professional body has no legal base. As a result, there is no accreditation process regulating the entry of the professionals. Also, the code of ethics remains mostly a pledge and not a compulsive obligation. Despite engaging in popularising the professional literature, in strengthening the training base and in bringing together into one fold all those engaged directly or indirectly with any branch of activity in personnel; the professional body i.e. NIPM is yet to go a long way in really professionalising personnel. Thus, in terms of its features the personnel profession has not reached full-fledged professional status.

Evaluating the Personnel Profession by the Clientele Served

The size and structure of the clientele served by a profession indicates the degree of professionalisation it has achieved. Personnel professionals serve business and industrial organisations only as a part of the management team employed by such organisations. Outside the employing organisation, their expertise and specialistion is of little use. Whereas, the medical professionals besides serving in organisational setting can extend their expertise to any setting. The diagnosis and treatment such medical experts give holds credence anywhere. Similarly, a legal professional's expertise also holds good in any setting. Such a universal application of the personnel professional's skill cannot be established.

However, another set of personnel professionals who take up consultancy in human resources management, pursue labour law practice and serve as officers in the Government labour departments as labour law implementations and evaluation authority serve a relatively larger clientele. Any individual worker, union, employer or organisation can seek the expertise assistance of these professionals as clients. But, even these personnel professional cannot be equated with the medical or legal professional in terms of universal application of their specialised knowledge. Thus, in comparison to the established professions, the personnel profession has achieved very less degree of professionalisation because of the limited size and structure of clientele it serves.

By explaining this position within the conceptual framework of local and cosmopolitan professionals, important inferences can be drawn. The personnel profession is mostly a local profession, whereas medicine and law can be attributed cosmopolitan nature. The reason is that the personnel profession, provides less scope for dynamism among its professionals. The pseudo-scientific discipline base contributed by the lack of clinical approach, further creates difficulty in validating the expertise in any setting. The scope, hence, to serve the profession is limited. And personnel activities mostly get bound by organisational dictates. In this way personnel is a local profession.

It is, however, pertinent to observe that few personnel professionals achieve high degree of professionalism. This is an evidence of personnel excellence of individual incumbents; but not of the professional ecology. Parallels of the American 'Percy-the personnel' are to be found among the Indian personnel executives who end up as corporate heroes. But their genre is an exception. It is true that the degree of professionalism varies from one incumbent to the other in every profession. But taking into account the professionalism achieved by the majority of professionals, personnel has a lot to improve.

From the above comparative analysis a theorisation explaining the locus standi of one profession in juxtaposition to other professions can be made. One set of professionals namely legal practitioners and private consultants may serve individuals, organisations or society independently. The second set of professionals can serve individual, organisation and society only as employees of an organisation. The third set of professionals serve only organisations by being employees of the same organisation. Personnel fall largely in the third category because majority of the professionals choose a career in organisations rather than in private consultancy.

The organisational bounds on the personnel profession create typical problems in professional-client relationship. Judging personnel by this client-professional relationship, it can be inferred that the personnel profession is not having the degree of freedom enjoyed by either the medical or legal professions. The organisations as clients never go to the personnel professional. Rather, the professionals are procured and inducted into the organisations as employees ostensibly for their skill. The expertise skill and knowledge of these professionals do not have decisive forcefulness—a weakness perpetuated by the staff position ascribed to personnel. It is the organisation as a client which decides and demands execution by the personnel professionals. In this way, the personnel profession does not qualify to be called as a full-fledged profession.

Evaluating the Personnel Profession by Its Elitist Status

The specialised service rendered by the professionals to the society the benefits accrued out of such service is reciprocated by allowing the professionals to exert great influence, to enjoy greater power and status in the society. All these contribute to their elitist position. The personnel professionals and their services being relevant to and bound by organisations which they serve; relatively enjoy a marginal status as elitists. They cannot be equated with the medical or legal professionals. Nor do they have anything extra from their other managerial counterparts to claim elitist status. Their skill being not totally relevant to larger social needs, their elitist status is in question. The trend that the occupational status often decides the social status, to some extend, compensates the dubious elitist nature of personnel profession. In this respect, however, the entire management profession finds itself in similar situation. The current professional status of personnel when placed on the professionalisation continuum of Carr-Saunders and Wilson, reveal that by all parameters the personnel profession has made a move towards the new profession stage from the would be profession stage in which Saunders placed personnel in 1933. In this process it has already crossed the semi-professional stage. The stage of old and established profession is still to be reached by personnel.

PART – II

PREDICTING THE FUTURE OF PERSONNEL PROFESSION IN INDIA

With regard to the future of personnel profession the projections need to be done by standing at the threshold of present status of the profession. As an occupation personnel has come to stay for its utility in organisations. It provides a philosophy to management action is a foregone conclusion. It has incorporated features of a profession, tried to professionalise itself since its very inception are all facts of past. Under influence of industrialization, technological advancement; changing attitudes and aspirations of work-force; trade unionism; government concern for welfarism and concommitant labour legislations; the personnel profession has found challenges enriching its content. Yet, from the evaluations made so far, the professional status of personnel currently is that it is not comparable to other established, full-fledged professions. This can conclusively be inferred from the immaturity found in its features, from the limited clientele it serves and from its restricted elitist status.

In this context, the future of personnel profession is attempted to be predicted by resorting to two approaches. First, the observations made by the personnel executives about the future prospects of personnel in India in the questionnaire are content analysed. Second, taking into account the changing trends in the ecology of the personnel profession as well as its inherent nature predictions are made.

A total of 240 respondents out of the sample of 255 (94 per cent) gave their predictions about the future prospects of personnel profession. A bleak and/or no future for the profession was predicted by 19 respondents. Of them four have given casual remarks. The rest fifteen have given analytical explanations in support of their negative opinion. The explanations advanced in this regard are quite varied as evident from the following:

— Functional jurisdiction of personnel is narrowed down due to the erosion by emerging new functionaries.

— The organisations are using personnel as decorative pieces doing odd jobs as they consider them unproductive.

— Unqualified professionals who lack specialised skill are rampant in organisations bringing disrepute to the profession.

— The mushroom growth of institutes not only stifle quality but also in the absence of uniform education and training base, contribute to the poor quality of professionals being turned out.

— Importance given to the line managers leaves less professional freedom for personnel. Importance of human resources as it is not realised, the personnel profession also is not given the importance due to it.

— Over-legislation, excessive dose of protection to the employees, multiplicity and militancy of trade unions, technological changes, capital-orientation of industry cause serious threat to the existence of the profession.

— While HRD is not a panacea for all problems faced by personnel, it is really not recognised as a profession.

Around thirty per cent (74 out of 255) of the respondents made positive remark quite casually stating that the future prospects of personnel profession is bright. They have not assigned any specific logic for their observation. On the other hand a large group 147 respondents accounting for around 58 per cent have visualised a bright future for personnel profession. But they have subjected their prediction to certain conditions to change and improve. They are enumerated below:

— Change and improvement in the discipline base by greater interaction between the academic institutes and organisations and improvement in the role of academic institutes in providing a uniform training base.

— Change and improvement in the role of organisations in providing the support system for the prospects of personnel profession like resolving line-staff misunderstanding and providing equity status to personnel on par with other managerial personnels.

— Improvement in the role of the Government and in the sociocultural and political system which would recognize human resources as a national resource and its planning and management a national policy, programme and practice.

— Improvement in the role of the personnel executives in terms of exhibiting effectiveness of their profession.

— Improvement in the role of the professional body (NIPM) in the areas of research and orientation programmes and elimination of non-professionals.

— Growth in industry; in technology; concomitant changes in the attitudes, skill and aspirations of the labour force; as conditions contributory to the growth and expansion of personnel profession.

— Changing trends like use of computers, emergence of HRM/HRD policies and practices, and impact of behavioural sciences as conducive towards the growth and enrichment of personnel profession.

Two sets of opinions with their logical explanations are equally relevant to the predictions made about the future of the personnel profession. The pessimism expressed by those who do not see a bright future for personnel profession base their logic on the past failures and prevailing unconducive conditions. The optimists on the other hand taking cue from the past and present make suggestions whose compliance, they argue, would contribute to a bright future for personnel profession. From this analogy it can be inferred that with the existing conditions continuing further the profession would not improve itself. So, changes are imperative. It is easy always to identify areas of change but not to bring them.

In this context a dispassionate speculation over the future status of personnel profession should always begin with the question that, 'what conditions in the personnel profession should be considered as a bright prospect ? The obvious answer to this question will be that, the personnel profession from its current status should reach the stages of old, established professions by enriching its features, by serving a larger clientele and thereby enjoying a higher elitist status in the society.

After reaching this stage, the personnel profession like any other profession would find new changes and challenges demanding enrichment of its inherent quality. At that stage it would join the band-wagon of the few established professions and become socially highly relevant. All these prospects would accrue, however, only after it would achieve the full-fledged professional status which can be hoped for.

India is a vast country endowed with rich natural resources. It has embarked upon modernisation through industrialization. Advancement in science and technology are spectacular. Yet, the country is based is faced with problems of economic development such as heavy foreign debt, foreign exchange crisis, balance of payment which are indicative of a poverty stricken economy. Productivity in every sector despite huge investments is not fully realised. Rising population enhances domestic needs which are not adequately met by the internal sources. Thus, all the economic development programmes in the country have failed to improve the economy. As against the background, the hugeness of its human resources which is quite untapped as indicated by the rampant unemployment and under employment, marked the resources is gradually realised. This culminated in the emergence of Human Resources Development (HRD) policy. To-day, India reposes its faith in its human resources whose availability is abundant but quality is poor. Enhancing the quality of manpower and its proper utilisation are the futuristic hopes of the country. In this regard, the personnel profession should find greater scope for being socially relevant and economically contributory.

The HRD policy which started in mid-eighties has as its objective concomitant growth of human potential alongwith the advancements in information technology, expansion of industrialization and use of artificial intelligence mechanisms like computers. This can rightly be called the beginning of a transitory phase towards a new awakening of realising the asset value of human resources.

The personnel profession in this context can break the shackles of its being local profession serving specifically industrial organisations. Because, more than on the capital which is in short supply, the entire hope, aspirations and future of India lie on its human resources. The profession can over-ridingly be relevant to the entire society irrespective of sectoral, organisational variances. At the macro level policies and programmes, vocational education and training can be the content of the personnel profession alongwith planning for creating avenues of employment so as to make use of the help of behavioural sciences, computers and improved human resources management techniques can ensure best utilisation of the human resources. These possibilities, can be realised however, when the profession makes itself capable of accepting the changes and challenges ahead of it.

The preparedness of the profession is a joint of many. Normally the professionals are held singularly responsible for the failure of profession as evident from the opinions of the personnel executives or from the observations made by researchers. But the contention here is that the professionals cannot make the profession relevant to new changes and challenges, unless supported by a conducive ecology.

The roles of the Government, the organisations, the academic institutes, the professional body obviously help or hinder the professional's excellence. The new role ordained for each one of these actors who provide the ecological support to the personnel profession can be defined in a suggestive framework.

The Government can enact a legislation for personnel profession on the lines of the Indian Medical Council Act and the Advocates Act. The Act *inter alia* should prescribe the specific qualification of professionals, accreditation programmes for entry into the profession and code of ethics by which the professionals will be bound. In order to implement the Act, professional body of the type of Medical Council and Bar Council can be framed under the law. Restrictions on the academic institutions in terms of the course structures, training methods, quality of instructions can be set in the law to have uniform training base. The accreditation programme becomes imperative, despite such restrictions because the concurrent practical experience to the personnel profession is difficult to give as part of the course curriculum. The Government by taking these steps will ensure a steady supply of quality professionals, a list of which can be kept as a pool from where organisations are bound to recruit. The Government can also rename the profession from 'Personnel' to 'Human Resources

Management/Development' in order to make it broad based. Once this Act is enacted, the provision of Welfare Officer provided in different legislations should be deleted as those provisions would become redundant. The law, however, should not prescribe the duties of the professionals because of the variant nature of the organisational needs and expectations.

The organisations as a part of their role should redefine the personnel job. In this process the extended functions or the non-personnel functions currently assigried are to be strictly kept outside the jurisdiction of the personnel. The diffusion of the core areas namely, personnel administration, industrial relations and labour welfare as specialised branches of activities alongwith some new specialisations splintering out of the personnel function like training and development can be declared as specialised activities. Such a multiplication of specialisations under an exalted nomenclature of HRM can be helpful in decentralization and better administration. For this purpose, specialisation in such areas after acquiring a common degree (as in case of medicine) can be prescribed as qualification. While treating them as part of the management team, these professionals should be assigned organisational status on par with other managerial functionaries. The line-staff division should need a restructuring wherein the personnel professionals could enjoy more decision making freedom in the areas of HRM policies and practices. These professionals with their expertise should restrain line managers in the art of HRM. Studying and analysing typical organisational conditions in HRM should be encouraged and supported by the organisations as an important functional area of HRM. Action research involving academicians in solving the organisational problems should also be encouraged by the organisations.

The restrictions put by law would obviously stop the mushroom growth of institutes. Instead of being either a part of general management course or a special paper in social work school, the HRM degree would be a specialised degree. Besides following the dictates of law in terms of course curricula, teaching methods and aids, the academic institutions would engage in a constant interaction with the organisations. This would enhance the quality of the discipline by bringing together the theory and practice and advancement in both. The HRM literature would be culture specific and innovate ways and measures suitable to the typical conditions prevailing in the Indian organisations.

The professional body from its current status of a voluntary body would find a more important regulative role because of its legal status. Besides maintaining accreditation programmes regulating the entry of the professionals, it would act as a disciplining forum for those who do not abide by the code of ethics prescribed under law. It would in its objectives bring together the practitioners and academicians under one fold of professionalism thereby enriching the discipline base.

Thus the personnel profession with the above suggestions would have a new found status a full-fledged profession. How long it will take to achieve these results is dependent on how quickly the Government responds to its role of enacting the law guiding the profession and others taking cue in responding to their new found roles. The NIPM can with its current collective strength can immediately take the initiative to realise the suggestions made above in reality.

With this sort of changed support system, the personnel professionals would find that they are required to adjust with a new environment. In this process of adaptation the personnel professionals should get rid of the mental blockade in which they find themselves on account of their past experiences and should cope with the new challenges and changes. However, quite contrary to the popular notion, it is reiterated here that the personnel professional is only a product of the professional ecology and even as a group they cannot change the professional status single handedly.

The suggestions made above may appear quite ambitious taking into account the position of personnel profession in U.K. and U.S.A. But, the logic for having such drastic steps in India is that it is not comparable to the countries like U.K. and U.S.A. who are technologically more developed, skill-wise their manpower is well trained and economically they are affluent. For India, undoubtedly the human resource is the only asset. This contention perhaps holds good for all developing countries. So the HRM profession should be improved by bringing about such drastic changes.

Bibliography

Agarwal, R.D. *Dynamics of Personnel Management in India — A Book of Readings*, Bombay, Tata McGraw Hill Publishing Co. Ltd., 1973.

Alexander, K. C., "Reorient Personnel Management," *Integrated Management*, May, 1969.

--------*Participative Management, The India Experience*, New Delhi, Sri Ram Centre for Industrial Relations and Human Resources, 1972.

Andrews, K.R., "Towards Professionalism in Business Management", *Harvard Business Review*, March-April, 1969.

Appley, L.A., *Management in Action : The art of getting things done through people*, Bombay, The Times of India Press, 1965.

Babbage, Charles, *On the Economy of Machinery and Manufaturers*, London, Charles Knight, 1832.

Barbar, Bernard, Is American Business Becoming Professionalised ? In Edward, A. Tiryakien Ed, *Sociological Theory*, New York, Harper and Row, 1967, pp. 212-145.

Baviskar, B. S., *The Politics of Development, Sugar Cooperatives in Rural Maharastra*, Delhi, Oxford University Press, 1971.

Beach, Dale S, *Personnel — The Management of People at Work*, New York, MacMillan Co., 1965.

Beeks, Gertrude, "The New Profession", *National Civic Federation Review*, Vol. 1 (Feb, 1, 1905).

Billimoria, R. P. "The Future Role of Personnel Officers' in J.A. Panakal, et al, Eds., *IIPM Readings in Personnel Management*, New Delhi. Orient Longmans, 1970.

BloomField, Meyer, "A New Profession in American Industry", in Daniel BloomField Ed., *Selected Articles on Employment Management*, New York, H. W. Wilson Co., 1919.

Bottomore, T. B., "Elites and Society", in G. Duncan Mitchell Ed., A *Dictionary of Sociology*, London, Routledge and Kegan Paul, 1968.

Brandies, Louls D., *Business - a Profession*, Boston, Small Maynard and Company, 1914.

Breach, E. F. L. ed., *The Principles and Practices of Management*, London, Longmans, Green and Company Ltd., 1963.

Burk, Samual L. H., "The Personnel Profession — Its Present and Future Status", Personnel Organisation and Professional Development, *Personnel Series*, No. 14, New York, American Management Association, 1943.

Carr-Saunders, Alexander Moris and P. A. Wilson, *The Professions*, Oxford, Clarindon Press, 1953.

Chatterjee, N. N. *Management of Personnel in Indian Enterprises*, Calcutta, Allied Book Agency, 1978.

Cogan, Moris, L. *Harvard Education Review*, 1953.

Copping, P. and Pickless, C., "Who goes into Personnel ?", *Personnel Executive*, October, 1981.

Cowan, Nick, "Change and the Personnel Profession", *Personnel Management*, January, 1988.

Dale, Earnest, *Organistion*, Bombay, D. B. Taraporevala & Sons, 1975.

Das, R. K., *Collective Bargaining in India*, New Delhi, Discovery Publishing House, 1988.

Davar, R. S., *Personnel Management and Industrial Relations in India*, New Delhi, Vikas Publishing House Pvt. Ltd., 1976.

Dayal, Iswar, "Role of Personnel in Organisation", *Indian Journal of Industrial Relations*, Vol. 5, No, 3 January, 1970.

Dolke, A. M. "Factors in job satisfaction in Indian Workers" in S. K. Roy and A. S. K. Menon Eds., *Motivation and Organisational Effectiveness*, New Delhi, Sri Ram Centre for Industrial Relations and Human Resources, 1974.

Drucker, Peter, F., "Personnel Management — Its assets and Liabilities", *Dun's Review and Modern Industry*, Vol. 63 No. 2314, June, 1954.

-----------*The Practice of Management*, London, Mercury Books, 1961.

Elibirt, Honry, "The Development of Personnel Management in the United States", *Business History Review*, Vol. 33, (Autumn, 1959).

Etzioni, Amitai, *Modern Organisations*, New Delhi, Prentice Hall of India Pvt. Ltd., 1965.

Flexner, Abraham, "Is Social Work a Profession ?", *School and Society*, June 20, 1915.

Flippo, E. B., *Principles of Personnel Management*, Tokyo, McGraw Hill Kogakusha, 1976.

French, Wendell, *The Personnel Management Process*, Boston, Houghton, Mifflin Co., 1964.

Ganguli, H. C., *Industrial Productivity and Motivation*, Bombay, Asia Publishing House, 1961.

--------*Structure and Process of Organisation*, Bombay, Asia Publishing House, 1964.

George, Claude, S. (Jr.), *The History of Management Thought*, New Delhi, Prentice Hall of India Pvt. Ltd., 1974.

Gouldner, A. W., "Cosmopolitan and Locals : Towards an analysis of Latent Social Roles-I", *Administrative Science Quarterly*, Vol. 2, 1957-58.

Government of India, *Report of Royal Commission on Labour in India. (1931)*, New Delhi, Agricole Publishing Academy, 1983 (Reprint).

Government of India, *Report of the Labour Investigation Committee*, New Delhi, 1944.

--------*Report of National Commission on Labour*, New Delhi, Ministry of Labour, 1969.

--------*Economic Survey, 1989-90*, New Delhi, Ministry of Finance 1990.

--------*Performance Budget, 1987-88*, New Delhi, Ministry of Labour, 1988.

Greenwood, Ernest, "Attributes of a Profession", *Social Work*, Vol. 2, July, 1957.

Harbison, F. and Myers, C. A., *Management in the Industrial World: An International Analysis*, New York, McGraw Hill Book Co., Inc., 1959.

Henstridge, J., "Personnel Management — A Frame Work for Analysis", *Personnel Review*, Vol. 4, No. 1, 1975.

Hunter, G., *The Role of Personnel Officer*, London, Institute of Personnel Management 1957.

Jacob, K. K., *Personnel Management in India — A study of Training and Functions of Personnel Officers*, Udaipur, S. J. C. Publications, 1973.

Kamat, R.S., "How Personnel Management can be more Dynamic ?", *Capital*, Vol. 12, 1970.

Kapoor, S. D., "The Extent of Job Satisfaction Among Indian Industrial Workers — A Normative Study", *Journal of India Academy of Applied Psychology*, Vol. 5, No. 1, 1968.

Kast, F. E., and Rosenzweig, James, E., *Organisaton and Management a systems and Contingency Approach*, New York, McGraw Hill Book Company, Inc., 1985.

Koontz, H. and O'Donell, C., *Essentials of Management*, New Delhi, Tata McGraw Hill Publishing Co., Ltd., 1978.

Kudchedkar, L. S., *Aspects of Personnel Management and Industrial Relations*, New Delhi, Tata McGraw Hill Publishing Co. Ltd., 1979.

Lambert, Richard, D., *Workers Factories and Social Change in India*, Bombay, Asia Publishing House, 1963.

Legge, K, and Exley, M., "Authority, Ambiguity and Adaptation: The Personnel Specialist's Dilemma", *Industrial Relations Journal*, Vol. 6 No. 3, 1975.

--------*Power, Innovation and Problem Solving in Personnel Management*, London, McGraw Hill, 1978.

Ling, Cyrll Curtis, *The Management of Personnel Relations, History and Origins*, Illinois, Richard D. Irwin Inc., 1965.

Manning, K., "The Rise and Fall of Personnel", *Management To-day*, March, 1983.

McFarland, Dalton, E., *Personnel Management: Theory and Practice*, London, Macmillan Company Ltd., 1969.

Memoria, C. B., *Labour Problems and Social Welfare in India*, Allahabad, Kitab Mahal, 1966.

Mhetras, V. G., *Labour Participation in Management: An Experiment in Industrial Democracy in India*, Bombay, Manaktalas, 1966.

Miller, F. B., "The Personnel Dilemma : Profession or not ?", *Personnel Journal*, Vol. 38, No. 2, June, 1959.

"Why I am for Professionalising ?", *Personnel Journal* Vo. 38, No. 3, July-August, 1959.

Millerson, G., *The Qualifying Associations*, London, Routledge and Kegan Paul, 1964.

Miner, John B., "Levels of Motivation to Manage among Personnel and Industrial Relations Managers", *Journal of Applied Psychology*, 61, No. 4, 1976.

Miner, John B. and Miner, Mary Green, *Personnel and Industrial Relations —A Managerial Approach*, New York, MacMillan Publishing Co. Inc., 1977.

Mitchell, G. D. and Ed., *A Dictionary of Sociology*, London, Routledge and Kegan Paul, 1968.

Mohanty, Girishbala, *A text Book of Industrial and Organisational Psychology*, New Delhi, Oxford and IBH Publishing Co, 1983.

Mohapatro, A. K. and Patro, G. C. *Managing Manpower at Work*, New Delhi, Discovery publishing House, 1989.

Monappa, Arun & Saiyadin, M. S., *Personnel Management*, New Delhi, Tata McGraw Hill Publishing Complany, 1979.

Moore, W. E. and Feldman, A. S. Eds., *Labour Commitment and Social Change in Developing Societies*, New York, Social Science Research Council, 1960.

Morris, Morris, D., *The Emergency of an Industrial Labour Force in India, A study of the Bombay Cotton Mills, (1854-1947)*, Bombay, Oxford University press, 1965.

Moorthy, M. V., *Principle of Labour Welfare*, Visakhapatnam, Gupta Brothers, 1968.

Murty, B. S., *Profiles of Indian Trade Unions: A study in Orissa*, Delhi, B. R. Publishing Corporation, 1986.

Myers, Charles, A., *Labour Problems in the Industrialistion of India* Combridge, Mass: Harvard University Press, 1958.

Myers, C. A. and Kannappan, S., *Industrial Relations in India*, Bombay, Asia Publishing House, 1970.

National Institute of Labour Management, *A Study of Personnel Officers in Greaters Bombay*, Bombay, The Author, 1966.

Nester, Oscar, W., *A History of Personnel Administration (1890-1910)*, Ph. D. Dissertation, University of Pennysilvania, 1954.

Ornati, Oscar, A., *Jobs and Workers in India*, Ithaca, Cornell University, 1955.

Pande, R. S., *The position and responsibilities of the Personnel Department within an undertaking in India*, Geneva, I. L. O., Labour Management Series, No. 7, 1960.

Patro, G. C., *Human Resources Management*, Delhi, Discovery publishing House, 1989.

Poduval, P. R. Organisational Effectiveness: A systems perspective in S. K. Roy and A. S. K. Menon Eds., *Motivation and Organisational Effectiveness*, New Delhi, Sri Ram Centre for Industrial Relations and Human Resources, 1974.

Prasad, L., *Personnel Management and Industrial Relations*, Bombay, Progressive Co-operation Pvt. Ltd., 1973.

Punekar, S. D., "The Personnel Manager in India ", *Industrial Relations*, Vol. XXV, No. 2, March-April, 1973.

Punekar, S. D., Deodhar, S. B. Sankaran, S., *Labour Welfare, Trade Unionism and Industrial Relations*, Bombay, Himalaya Publishing House, 1981.

Ramswamy, E. A., *The Worker and His Union (A study in South India)*, Bombay, Allied Publishers, 1977.

--------*Industry and Labour : An Introduction*, Delhi, Orford University Press, 1981.

Rath, Gopal, C., *The Welfare Officer in Indian Industry*, M. S. Dissertation, Cornell University (Unpublished), 1956.

Rath, B. P., *Industrial Relations and Participative Management*, New Delhi, Deep and Deep Publications, 1989.

Reilley, Ewing, W., "The Opportunity and the Challenge of Personnel Administration " in Robert E. Finley, *The Personnel Man and his Job*, Bombay, D. B. Taraporevala and Co. Pvt. Ltd., 1962.

Ritzer, George and Trice, Harrison M., *An Occupation in Conflict ! A study of the Personnel Manager*, New York, State School of Industrial and Labour Relations, Cornell, University, 1969.

Ritzer, George, "The Professionals ; Will Personnel Occupations Ever become Professionals ?" *The Personnel Administration*, Vol, 16:3, 1971.

Roy, S. K., *Management in India : New Perspectives*, Meerut, Meenakshi

Prakashan, 1974.

Roy, S. K. and A. S.K. Menon, Eds., *Motivation and Organisational Effectiveness*, New Delhi, Sri Ram Centre for Industrial Relations and Human Resources, 1974.

Rudrabasavaraj, M. N. *Personnel Administration in India*, Poona, Baikuntha Mehta National Institute of Cooperative Management, 1969.

Saxena, R. C., *Labour Problems and Social Welfare*, Meerut, K. Nath & Co., 1986.

Scott, W. D., Clothier, R. C., *Personnel Management*, New York, McGraw Hill, 1941.

Seth, N. R., "Trade Unions in an Indian Factory : A Sociological Analysis", *The Economic Weekly*, Vol. XII, No. 29 and 30, July 23, 1960.

--------*The Social Framework of an Indian Factory*, Bombay, Oxford University Press, 1968.

Sethi, N. K., *Management Perspectives*, Bombay, Progressive Cooperation Pvt. Ltd., 1972.

Sharma, Baldev, R., *The Indian Industrial Workers*, Delhi, Vikas Publishing House, 1974.

Sharma, G. K., *Labour Movement in India : Its Past and Present*, New Delhi, Sterling Publishers (P) Ltd., 1971.

Sinha, D., *Psychological Studies*, Patna Institute of Psychological Research and Service, Patna University, 1958.

Sinha, G. P. and Sinha P. R. N., *Industrial Relations and Labour Legislation*, New Delhi, Oxford and IBH Publishing Co., 1977.

Sinha, Jai B. P., "Psychological Background and Work Motivation" in S. K. Roy and A. S. K. Menon, Eds., *Motivation and Organisational Effectiveness*, New Delhi, Sri Ram Centre for Industrial Relaions and Human Resources, 1974.

Stanton, Erwin, S., "Last chance for Personnel to come of Age", The *Personnel Administrator*, 20:7 (1975).

Strauss, George and Sayles Leonard R., *Personnel the Human Problems of Management*, New Delhi, Prentice Hall of India Pvt. Ltd., 1968.

Subraminiam, K. N., *Labour Management Relations in India*, New Delhi, Asia Publishing House, 1967.

Sur, Mary, Ed., *Personnel Management in India : The Practical Approach to Human Relations in Industry*, Bombay, Asia Publishing House, 1973.

Tandon, Prakash, *Professional Management in India — Its Potential and Problems*, Ludhiana, Punjab Agriculture University Press, 1974.

Tarneja, R. S. *Personnel Mangers at Work*, Madras, Human Resources Foundation, 1968.

Taylor, F. W., *Principles of Scientific Management*, New York, Harper and Brothers, 1911.

Tead, Ordway, "Personnel Administration", *Encyclopaedia of the social Services*, Vol. 12, 1934.

Thurley, K., "Personnel Mangement in the U. K. — a Case for Urgent Treatment ?" *Personnel Management*, August , 1981.

Tiwari, Y. K., Trade Union in India : Changes and Accountability in J. C. Rastogi, P. P. Arya and S. D. Tripathy, Eds., *Planning for Industrial Relations Management — A 21st Centrury Perspective*, New Delhi, Deep and Deep Publications, 1987.

Tyagi, B. P., *Economics and Social Welfare*, Meerut, Jayaprakash Nath & Co., 1986.

Tyson, S., *Specialistss in Ambiguity : Personnel Management as an Occupation*, Ph. D. Thesis, London University, 1979.

Tyson, Shaun and Fell Allan, *Evaluating the Personnel Function*, London, Hutchinson Personnel Management Series, 1986.

Ure, Androw, *The Philosophy of Manufacturers*, London Charlesknight, 1835.

Vaid, K. N., *The Labour Welfare Officer*, Delhi School of Social Work, 1962.

--------*Papers on Absenteeism*, New Delhi, Asia Publishing House, 1967.

--------*Labour Welfare in* India, New Delhi, Sri Ram Centre for Industrial Relations and Human Resources, 1970.

Vollmer, H. M. and Mills, Donald L., Eds., *Professionalisation*, Englewood Cliffs, New Jersey, Prentice Hall Inc., 1966.

Watson, T. J., *The Personnel Managers*, London, Routledge and Kegan Paul, 1977.

Wilensky, H. L., "The Professionalisation of Everyone ?", *American Journal of Sociology*, September 6, 1954.

Wilking S., Vincent, "The Status of Today's Personnel Man" in Robert E. Finely Ed., *The Personnel Man and His Job*, Bombay, D. B. Taraporevala & Co. Pvt, Ltd., 1962.

Yoder Dale, "Trends Towards Professionalisation in Personnel Work ", *Personnel Journal*, Vol. 28, No. 9, February, 1950.

--------*Personnel Principles and Policies*, Englewood Cliffs, New Jersey, Prentice Hall Inc., 1952.

--------et at., *Handbook of Personnel Management and Labour Relations*, New York, McGraw Hill Book Co. Inc., 1958.

Index